# The Theatre of Naturalism

# Currents in Comparative Romance Languages and Literatures

Tamara Alvarez-Detrell and Michael G. Paulson
*General Editors*

Vol. 185

PETER LANG
New York • Washington, D.C./Baltimore • Bern
Frankfurt • Berlin • Brussels • Vienna • Oxford

*Philip Beitchman*

# The Theatre of Naturalism

## *Disappearing Act*

**PETER LANG**
New York • Washington, D.C./Baltimore • Bern
Frankfurt • Berlin • Brussels • Vienna • Oxford

**Library of Congress Cataloging-in-Publication Data**
Beitchman, Philip.
The theatre of naturalism: disappearing act / Philip Beitchman.
p. cm. — (Currents in comparative Romance languages and literatures; v. 185)
Includes bibliographical references and index.
1. Naturalism in literature. 2. Drama—19th century—History and criticism.
3. Drama—20th century—History and criticism. I. Title.
PN1650.N38B45    808.2'912—dc22    2010030794
ISBN 978-1-4331-1297-3
ISSN 0893-5963


Bibliographic information published by **Die Deutsche Nationalbibliothek**.
**Die Deutsche Nationalbibliothek** lists this publication in the "Deutsche
Nationalbibliografie"; detailed bibliographic data is available
on the Internet at http://dnb.d-nb.de/.

The paper in this book meets the guidelines for permanence and durability
of the Committee on Production Guidelines for Book Longevity
of the Council of Library Resources.

∞

© 2011 Peter Lang Publishing, Inc., New York
29 Broadway, 18th floor, New York, NY 10006
www.peterlang.com

Printed in Germany

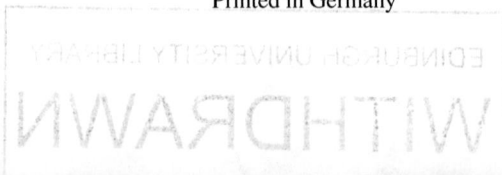

"Vivre?  Les serviteurs feront cela pour nous."

—Axël

# Contents

# Acknowledgments

I wish to thank, first of all, *Daniel Gerould* for his many helpful comments and suggestions on an earlier draft, and especially for his frankness and honesty, helping me, through his profound knowledge of theatre history, to 'fact-check' my text, as well as clarify my ideas and intentions. I wish also to thank *Tom Bissinger*, for the sympathy and intelligence of his reflections and conversation as this project developed. I wish to express my gratitude to *Kenneth Brown* for the kindness of his very informative reading of the chapter about his play *The Brig* and *The Living Theatre*, and for email and telephone communications shedding light on these subjects; to *Richard Schechner* for his helpful and knowledgeable comments about this chapter; to *Steven Ben Israel*, for a pleasant afternoon 'hanging out' with him, affording me an insider's glimpse of "a day in the life" of *The Brig*, from the point-of-view of a key player (and others he knew in that cast of 'prisoners and guards', some so soon to be political fugitives) in that revolutionary (lets not mince words!) performance event; to The New York Public Research Libraries, for access to their great collections as well as for allowing me the privileges of shelf and work space at the Wertheim Study there; to *Caitlin Lavelle*, Acquisitions Editor at Peter Lang, whose enthusiasm for my work was so decisive for me to publish there, and to *Jackie Pavlovic*, Production Supervisor, for the generosity of her careful and caring attention to detail. I owe a special debt of gratitude to *Mick Stern*, not only for the witty wisdom of his insightful reading and abundant comments but also for his invaluable assistance in technical matters. Lastly, no one has done more to further this project than *Marjorie Gamso*, dancer, choreographer, writer, extraordinary reader and very special friend...Chapter IX ("Neutron Bomb of the Mind: a Digression on Stiegler") has been posted, in an earlier version, on two French websites: 1) interpc.fr ("Interzone", managed by *Isabelle Aubert*, devoted to the work of William Burroughs); 2) robertredeker.fr (*Robert Redeker*, 'philosopher-in-exile', whose translator I'm proud to be).

# Introduction: Ushering in the Spectacle

Whatever its other associations and connotations, 'Naturalism' does summon up the image of an extreme realism in representation, a realism *theatre*, among the arts, for structural factors, would seem ideally suited to convey. Theatre was always already naturalistic well before Zola invented the genre of naturalistic theatre; while with Zola, naturalism, whether staged or in the novel, was as much about the culture, politics, and certainly about the "science" of its times as about the works themselves (begging the question there is such a thing). So we mean this study as both a selective historical overview of naturalistic theatre, beginning with Zola and continuing through Ibsen, Strindberg, Gorky and others, and still 'alive' if not maybe as well, but also as an exploration of its cultural, political and philosophical ramifications. A leitmotif of this work is that that the evolution of this type of theatre, in the direction of "hypernaturalism", as Hans-Thies Lehmann in *Postdramatic Theatre* (2006) calls its contemporary avatar (e.g. the grotesque[1] 'excess of miniscule reality' and/or routinization of cruelty in works of Werner Schwab, Kroetz, Fassbinder, Vinover and others), anticipates, paradoxically, a derealization, or virtualization that now permeates our 'society of the spectacle':

> What may have seemed to be Naturalistic in the theatre since 1970—probably also under the impression of photorealism—actually represents a form of derealization, not of perfection of reproduction. (Lehmann,116)

Representational fidelity may be rather an agent of effacement than of the enhancement; as Baudrillard noted, eerily, prophetically, in *Simulations* (1983) about the WTC:

> It is the duplication of the sign that destroys its meaning.... The two towers of the W.T.C. are the visible sign of the closure of the system in a vertigo of representation. (p. 136)

Lehmann, in fact, cites Baudrillard specifically in invoking *hypernaturalism*:

> [which is] is preferable [to Naturalism], as it makes reference to the concept of 'hyperrealism' that Baudrillard used to designate a non-referential, media produced, heightened resemblance of things to themselves, not the adequacy of images to the real. (117)

Imitation may be the sincerest form of flattery, yet when representation is too faithful, cloning its model, it verges on *parody*, so how indeed can the 'original' emerge unscathed, or even survive the operation?   Clearly therefore, some critical distance and suspicion will be called for in examining the effects, immediate and long run, and assaying the goals, stated and implied in this Theatre of Naturalism.  So it is that in these essays *theory will overlap with theatre*.  Pierre Legendre remarks "the close connection between terms of Greek provenance such as *theory and theatre*"[2], citing Pierre Chantraine's *Dictionnnaire étymologique de la langue grecque*, which we've consulted with the following results: *theatre*, strictly speaking, derives from the Greek *thea*, meaning "view, spectacle, contemplation" (p. 425), while *theory* descends from the Greek *theoroi*, anciently "persons sent to consult oracles, or to attend religious festivals"; while "from the time of Plato *theory* acquires the sense of 'contemplation, consideration' ...as opposed to practical matters" (p. 433). *Theatre*, then, etymologically-philosophically would involve the double distance of first of all the playwright's and the production team, then secondly the spectators viewing it; while with *theory*, there would be a third dimension, or triple distance, encompassing those who try to understand not only the spectacle but the spectators.  For both *theatre* and *theory* assume a place outside of the world they interpret, this "place outside" that is also a leitmotif in Samuel Weber's *Theatricality as Medium* (2004).

Naturalism, in its literary sense at least, which includes its theatrical one that is the focus here, was very much of French provenance[3], as is or was "theory".  So it's no coincidence that I reflect here on the relevance of this theatre in the light of French theory that has emerged since what I consider to be its last heyday—say with the late 50's and 60's Living Theatre productions of plays of Gelber and Brown, and the Royal Court (and New York) productions of such as Wesker and Storey—to figures like Baudrillard, Derrida, and Bernard Stiegler.  About Stiegler, an important presence recently, for instance, I found myself wondering at length what he would make retroactively of a moment of some very dramatic 'resistance to oppression', as presented in Kenneth Brown's *The Brig*,[4] of 1963, a watershed production of the Living Theatre, and for our culture generally, and, significantly, recently (2007) revived... Well before that, however, not much wondering is involved about the links between Marx and Engels' abundant commentary and clear enthusiasm over the Silesian Weaver's insurrection of the 1840's—its blatant connection, for example with the theory and the 'spirit' of the Communist Manifesto—*and* Hauptmann's later play and dramatic version of that event, *The Weavers* (1892), staged halfway between the Paris Commune and the Russian Revolution in politically turbulent Paris, and so central to the naturalist career of Antoine's Théâtre Libre. Comparably "class struggle" issues are central for the chapters on Ibsen's *Ghosts*, Strindberg's *Miss Julie*; Gorky's *Lower Depths*, Tolstoy's *The Power of Darkness*, Shaw's *Mrs. Warren's Profession* and Synge's *Riders to the Sea*.

Towards the more recent authors, Arnold Wesker, Kenneth Brown and David Storey, the approach will be by way of intervening developments in theory, principally French—examining the cogency, retroactively, for instance, of the 'classless' stances toward social change of such as B. Stiegler and Derrida (*Specters of Marx*) to what was certainly the 'revolutionary' mood of The Living Theatre's signature productions of *The Brig*, as well as, unavoidably, Jack Gelber's *The Connection*, of 1959[5]— ending up with reflections, centered on the theatre of David Storey, where it seems to me the background becomes the foreground, the stage and stage machinery—for instance changing room, tent, and asylum garden— becoming the subject—in the light of Jean Baudrillard's notions about the 'sliding' of the subject into the object, thereby ushering in an age when we see things 'from the side of the object'; then finally concluding with some remarks on the prospects for naturalism in particular and theatre in general in the context of the new technologies that present the same kind of challenge to 'realism' and 'spectacle' of the theatre that photography once presented to representation for painting...

An older study by the Marxist critic, Raymond Williams, *Drama from Ibsen to Brecht* (Oxford, 1971) focuses very largely on social and political factors, as we do here, covering much of the same ground also, but he casts a much wider net, since naturalism, which he views anyway as having been 'relayed' (shades of Hegel) by expressionism and other styles, is not at all privileged in his book; and of course, the impact of recent French theory would be missing from his work, though it does engage however the existentialism of such as Sartre.

There are of course studies of theatrical naturalism and also many studies that apply the insights of "theory" in various fields and disciplines, but none I know of that links theatrical naturalism specifically with theory generally. Samuel Weber's *Theatricality as Medium*, certainly links theory and theatre, but doesn't deal with naturalism, except in passing, and even then not as the catalytic political expression it has been... A seminal work of Robert Abirached, *La Crise du personnage dans le théâtre moderne* (1978), certainly crosses paths in many ways with my own; we seem, nevertheless, to be going in somewhat different directions; for his focus is not naturalist, but especially on expressionist, Brechtian, and theatre of cruelty (Artaud, of course) modes, where character and language are elided in favor of gesture and the 'gift' of the suffering body, consistent also with the influential depersonalization teachings of Edward Gordon Craig. Elinor Fuchs' study, *The Death of Character: Perspectives on Theater after Modernism* (Indiana, 1996), parallels my own theme of the *disappearing individual* in the naturalist theatre; but her work is focused on specifically experimental approaches, from expressionist to postmodern (for instance that of the Wooster Group), for which the dissolution of the subject is already a given, whereas I see it as very much still in process. Additionally she polarizes the "solid characters" of traditional theatre against their effacement (French theory helping) of recent times, while blunting, it seems to me, the radicality of her 'take' by suggesting this development is only a (welcome) return to Aristotelian strictures on "Music, Diction, Thought and Spectacle" (p. 176), too neglected in favor of Character; waxing even a bit mystical with a comforting allusion to Buddhist (*ibid*) anonymity! Similarly character-assaulting and plot-downplaying as Fuchs' (minus the 'mysticism') and my study is the above mentioned Lehmann's immensely influential *Postdramatic Theatre* (English translation, 2006), already a classic in the "performance" approach to contemporary theatre, relaying and supplementing (for Lehmann) the too narrow Brechtian 'epic theatre' bias (and of course crisis therein) of Peter Szondi's *Theory of Modern Drama* (English translation, 1986); but the novelty of my work would be to find these same drama-dissolving tendencies working in the very citadel of story, representation and character, the enemy camp as it were of the decried Naturalism, which, in fulfilling itself, or evolving in the direction of what Lehmann has called a "hypernaturalism" autodestructs, or auto-deconstructs itself, opening the way to the anonymity, ritual and rite of theatre-as-performance. Lehmann, after relating the term to Baudrillard's de-realizing *hyperreal*, noted its meaning for Jean-Pierre Sarrazac (*L'Avenir du drame*) as being:

> a Naturalism 'of the second degree'...the lower worlds take on the attraction of the exotic that is offered for consumption. (Lehmann, 117-118)

Also characteristic of this *hypernaturalism* is a definite coldness, cool, indifference or at least neutrality, a "de-pathization" (ibid, 118) discouraging audience identification with the characters—while sympathy or empathy was still possible or even encouraged by the older Naturalism (which as a matter of fact, Lehmann reminds us that Brecht had called derisively a "theatre of pity"!).

Perhaps closest in intent to this study is Baz Kershaw's *The Radical in Performance: Between Brecht and Baudrillard* (Routledge, 1999), a work that invokes, as mine does thematically, the theories of Baudrillard. He does so, it seems to me, however, in a polar sense, since he conceives Baudrillard—and the ideas he is taken to represent, whereby all of reality becomes virtual (illusion) and spectacle (theatre: if theatre is everywhere, as in the situationists' *Society of the Spectacle*, theatre is nowhere,) in their most extreme form—as a threat, a menace and a challenge to the very essence of theatre, if not its continued existence as such, a kind of 'death knell'. For Kershaw, Baudrillard's 'simulations' would leave no room for a play in a world which is already one...We see things in a more unitary way, or try to, as if whatever Baudrillard stood for—certainly, as for other important figures in French culture generally, Barthes, Foucault and Legendre—taking account of the assault on the subject and corresponding celebration of the object characteristic of 'late Capitalism'—was already working to undermine traditional conceptions of character and individuality long before anyone ever heard of Baudrillard, for instance in the plays of Kenneth H. Brown, Arnold Wesker and David Storey.

Finally a word is in order about the blatantly political, even proletarian way I invoke theatrical naturalism. Philosophically of course, the term Naturalism has always connoted empiricism, materialism, and generally that the world can be understood without resorting to notions fundamentally 'outside' it, like God, previous or future lives and suchlike (or that such notions would only obfuscate things); it is, if anything, anti-supernatural. In its theatrical avatar, which begins around 1870, around the time of the defeat of the Paris Commune, it is all of these things, but also conveys images, prospects and representations of a class struggle then surfacing as an increasingly unavoidable issue confronting humanity. Although the naturalism in the plays we treat here tends to embrace and convey the perspectives of an exploited, but energetic, resentful and dynamic underclass[6], proletarian and lower (lumpen) this should not be taken to suggest that something automatically connects naturalism with radical politics, however 'naturally' it works in that context. It has, after all, been easily adapted to middle class interests, supporting a self-satisfied and complacent view of reality, as apparently (and ironically) was the function it fulfilled in the Soviet Union in the twenties and thirties:

> For a long time Soviet theatre, as was the case for the other arts was forced into the mold of a narrow naturalism, and obliged to render reality only in a well laundered reproductions. The petit-bourgeois tradition, under the mask of a conventionalized Stanislavism had the upper hand[7].

A major purpose of ours here is to burnish and restore a conception of theatrical naturalism as a volatile, society-impinging, potentially dangerous and explosive mix, a way of theatre that was also a way of challenging the justice and inevitability of prevailing orders of regimentation and control, but one that had been clouded over, coopted by the forces of social atrophy, conservatism and incorporation by market ideology. In fact the image of naturalism currently is probably more bourgeois than proletarian, more reflecting the living rooms of Neil Simon without the subversive complexity of class violence (more or less openly manifest) in Ibsen and Shaw that undermine comforts there, much less the provocative reenactment of the street battles of Hauptmann *Weavers* or any display of the desperate resignation of the trapped denizens and transients in Gorky's *Lower Depths*.

Nor is the end here necessarily to resurrect, revive, or otherwise reinvigorate whatever naturalism has meant, in its sundry avatars and phases, in the more than a century since its dramatic debut, with Zola's watershed decision to try to efface the barrier between stage and audience, art and 'real life'. Not only what constitutes theatre today (and what does not?!), but also protest, dissent, and opposition, insofar as the arts, and here theatre conjure them up are now more complex, elusive phenomena than hitherto. Contemporary thinkers, even those with radical sympathies, tend to stress the futility of *direct* resistance to oppression. Zygmunt Bauman's recent work[8], for example, has been especially strident and eloquent about the 'employment' of resistance by the mercantile system that turns everything into grist for its mills, minting protest pamphlets into so many dollars. Paolo Virno, a key figure once in the Italian radical movements of the 60's and 70's of direct action resistance (Autonomia), and still very germane to our subject here, just as firmly now rejects direct expression of dissent, which he has come to regard as fighting on the terrain of the enemy, given that we are living in the aftermath of a 'defeated revolution'. He endorses instead the more effective ways of *exile*, taking as a model the Biblical flight from Egypt; or else simply *humor*, which is another kind of flight, but a mental and attitudinal one, as in the hilarious shifts in games of consciousness, embodied in Freud's book on jokes, whereby we obey, suddenly and subversively other rules of logical engagement.[9] Obviously more consistent with such ideas, would be a theatre like the absurdist, linguistically playful and hilarious one of Ionesco or even Beckett; or that of other productions (in other more adaptable mediums like film), or hybrid, multimedia, set in 'exotic' or fantastic times and places, which would have (already?) supplanted naturalism as more authentic oppositional events.

Jean Baudrillard, on the other hand, Hegelian in this respect as ever, endorses as valid (without being sanguine about its 'reforming' prospects) a resistance that pits life against life, that is that plays the death card of the oppositionist against the death card of the system. This is a theme that is remarkable for its constancy and endurance through the vicissitudes of his work, from the rallying cry of his early summum, *Symbolic Exchange and Death* (1976), where, for instance, indigenes are seen to be authentically registering their protest, attacking and weakening the system (shown to fail in its ambition to control and incorporate everyone and everything) by disappearing off the face of the earth (through voluntary self-starvation, refusal to procreate etc.) to the "18 Kamikazes" who are taken, in *L'Esprit du terrorisme* (2002, but first appearing in *Le Monde* as an article-essay on 3 November of 2001, or while the embers of the WTC were still smoldering...) to have forced our "empire" of a globalizing system to respond in the only way possible: through the suicide of the towers themselves, judging by the result, unquestionably a stupendously successful resistance action and counterattack; not to mention, by the standards of Capitalism's own values and logic, deploying an astoundingly 'profitable' outlay-profit ratio— trillions of dollars of damages, plus the 'morale' damages, for the investment of a few lives and not many more bucks!:

> The symbolic collapse of a whole system was effected through an unanticipated complicity, as if, in collapsing by themselves, committing suicide, the towers had entered into the game in order to perfect the event. (p. 14).

Accordingly, "back then" (early '60's), *when* The Living Theater was being hounded out of the country, because of the daring challenge they mounted to the military-industrial complex and the coming surveillance society with *The Brig*; and the gauntlet they threw down with *The Connection* and other provocations, for instance being busted for nudity in connection with their productions of *Paradise Now* in Rio or Philadelphia; *when* the producers, author and cast of Gorky's *The Lower Depths*, around 1900, were rewarded for their success not only with many curtain calls but long years of exile and/or imprisonment, *then* theatre could be seen, in Baudrillardian terms, as effectively and authentically oppositional, playing its skin, its life, against the system it's attacking. Alternatively, today, the creators of such iconoclastic productions, or revivals thereof, however competent and 'faithful', are no longer threatened with anything except possibly bankruptcy and poverty (no mean prospect, but still...) for their show. Given anyway, this theatralization of real life and vice-versa, so much a function of the virtual reality Baudrillard is credited with having invented, or at least named, any resistance worth the name would have moved over to the theatre real life has become, as in the (how many acts, starting with the *foreshadowing* of the earlier bombing of 1996?) 'tragedy' of the 9/11 attacks, whose heroes, or antiheroes (in the sense of Shakespeare's Iago or Marlowe's Barabas) conform so well to Aristotelian prescriptions as to recognized and chosen fates or destinies. Alas, where however is the *catharsis*, when not only the protagonists and agonists are done for, but also the very theatre is in flames[10], with its chorus (a cast of thousands), not to mention a huge chunk of the audience going up in smoke, or falls/jumps out of windows,[11] rather than walking calmly chanting out of the aisles, the way a chorus was supposed to have entered the same way onto the *skena* of a Greek theater, carrying tapers...?

Let's reconsider also this 'place apart' so intrinsic to the connected concepts of theatre and theory we began by reconnoitering, in terms of the questions the idea of the mere existence such a place now begs. In terms of time, when we're not working we're networking and or consuming or developing skills and aptitudes (like sociability) that make social life (in other words, for just about everyone, life) of any sort feasible.[12] In terms of *places* apart, on the other hand, if they're there at all, such spaces must be increasingly rare and difficult (if not expensive—in the sense of tourism) of access in a world in which work becomes interchangeable and one with 'leisure' and consumption. Places are increasingly privatized and rented, controlled, surveyed and subject to round-the-clock surveillance and control. Sheldon Wolin[13] laments the anti-democratic consequences of this (unquestionably) deliberate process:

> What is at stake here is the control of public space and the power to depict, to discourage and intimidate, and ultimately to filter what is happening and being expressed at a time when technology makes filtering relatively easy. Consider the attempts on the part of protest groups during the summer of 2004 to enter the public space of streets in the environs of the conventions of the two national parties.[14] As the police herded the protesters into the equivalent of cattle pens, the media presented the groups as bizarre and ignored the serious argument they were attempting to offer.. In effect the media transformed a political action, intended for the civic education of a public, into a spectacle framed for mass entertainment. (216)

To add a few logs to this fire, here in New York City we've recently privatized a very notable public space, Bryant Park, on 42nd Street between 5th and 6th Avenues, now being 'managed' by The Bryant Park Corporation—where it's nothing now but a year round cavalcade of Ice Skating, Fashion Shows, Concerts, and various spectacles—occasionally the spacious lawn is available for public relaxation of various sorts, like concerts and movies, with corporate sponsorship clearly in evidence, of course; but really, can anyone imagine a political rally or event taking place there, a protest or action, direct or not, of any sort?[15] Or take the so-called public spaces corporations have created for 'public use' as a part of an agreement with the city—say the very attractive one, with high ceilings and large bamboo trees, even little birds flying here and there, at the corner of 57th and Madison—is any organizing going to take place there under the watchful eye of omnipresent security and/or cameras? Even in terms of this 'real life' that has been turned into (only) theatre, the acknowledgement is inescapable that not only has 'real life' or what we mean by it changed in many ways, becoming the way theorists like Agamben and Foucault describe it rather "bare life", basically all that's left to humanity today; but the function and role of theatre correspondingly has shifted, probably right off the political stage or out of the arena. Where, for instance, is there an audience to be electrified or shocked into awareness and consciousness the way the insulted and dismayed English and American spectators of Ibsen (*Ghosts*) or Shaw (*Mrs. Warren's Profession*) once were, *a fortiori* the traumatized 'witnesses' of that preview of coming attractions of our 'surveillance society', *The Brig*, of The Living Theatre, run out of the country for their pains? Yes, we can 'bring back' the plays, more or less as they were written, but in different contexts they serve different purposes—or write new ones escalating the honesty and outrage (since we have become jaded with familiarity), now as likely no longer to challenge and defy a system, but in so many subtle and indirect ways to affirm, justify and *legitimize* it: whatever is wrong with 'the way things are' at least dissent and demurral is allowed to be represented, voiced if not really acted upon. Whether today you're turning real life into theatre or theatre into real life, in either case your job is done, once you've "voted" (i.e. attended some kind of progressive performance event), you're free to go about your business, and if you have none, you better turn whatever you're doing into one. You've done the best you can with the art (the genes) that's been handed to you, given the circumstances.

However, when has humanity ever been satisfied with being the product of circumstance, however consoling or useful such a notion must be at times; whether on stage, in the audience, in the aisle (even ushering!, or in the cashiers' booth), in front of the myriad screens we've turned our world over to? Finally we're going to wonder about what and who has brought these circumstances about. Then in the inner stage of our thoughts and dreams, we'll summon, like a genie out of Aladdin's lamp that most challenging of "The Ten Theses on Feuerbach" of Marx: "The materialist doctrine that men are products of circumstances...forgets that it is men that change circumstances."[16]

# I.   The Mirror Stage: *Thérèse Raquin*

And so art is everywhere, since artifice is at the very heart of reality. And so art is dead, not only because its critical transcendence is gone, but because reality itself, entirely impregnated by an aesthetic which is inseparable from its own structure, has been confused with its own image. Reality no longer has the time to take on the appearance of reality. It no longer even surpasses fiction: it captures every dream even before it takes on the appearance of a dream. Schizophrenic vertigo of these serial signs, for which no counterfeit, no sublimation is possible, immanent in their repetition—who could say what the reality is that these signs simulate?

—Jean Baudrillard[1]

I imagine this creator [of 'the new theatre'] overleaping the most carefully drawn limits, breaking all imposed frameworks, expanding the stage to the point it blends in totally with the auditorium, lending the spark of life to the painted trees of the aisles, and allowing freely the breeze of life to blow through the background scenery....Now the naturalists have come along to say, quite bluntly, that poetry is everywhere, in everything, and even rather more in the present and the real than in the abstract past. Every fact, at any time, has its poetic and superb side.

—Émile Zola[2]

Three actresses....perform separately before an enormous mirror in which the audience is reflected. The actresses complain that in today's post-Fordist society, there is no longer any such thing as 'backstage': The audience sits everywhere. There are no more places of retreat.

—Diedrich Diederichsen[3]

In the preface to his play, *Thérèse Raquin* (1873), adapted from his novel (1867) of the same name Zola explains several of his choices as rising from his efforts to break down the separation between public and stage, or between theatre and reality, a 'distance' that had always been there before: the lesser characters were purposely made "stupid and ineffective", so as to bring out "beneath the atrocious anguish of my heroes the banality of everyday life"; the purpose of the ordinary activities on the stage—like playing dominos, cleaning lettuce, eating soup (even arguing over too much salt in it!) was to convey the impression that the characters were not merely "'acting' but 'living' in front of the public."[4] Naturalism in theatre would therefore mean that the stage was to be real in a way that it had never been before, thus catching up to other arts (novel, painting) that that already learned their lessons from science. Modern theatre, in fact, needed a genius of the level of Shakespeare, Corneille or Molière who would do for the stage what Balzac had done for the novel.[5] Not that Zola was claiming that there was such a thing as 'progress' in the arts, but that they should reflect and communicate with their time—high tragedy was fine for the 16th and 17th centuries and romantic drama (Hugo) for the 1830's, but theatre today needed to reflect the empirical, social and economic predicaments and quandaries of humanity presently.

An art that is totally innovative, original and 'forward looking' would constitute, of course not only an aporia (language, for example, being always already there, not to mention color), attempting to realize which would constitute for the artist a catastrophe or tragedy of the sort Zola later was to limn in his novel about an idealistic and uncompromisingly original and therefore doomed painter,[6] L'Oeuvre (1886). Zola, on the other hand, was ready to compromise, maybe too ready; for as radical a departure in the direction of a naturalistic theatre as he meant his play to be, Zola would be careful to humor his public with as much tradition as he thought it required to tolerate its innovations. Whether Zola's own concessions in the matter of theatre were necessary or not, there is no question that they had an impact in just how experimental it was going to be. Accordingly, in his preface to the play Zola explains that the "poignancy of the situation" should compensate for the public's "hunger for a story", while creating toleration for the multitude of minute details he uses to create naturalistic verisimilitude [iii]. "Real life on the stage" must therefore be presented from "a point-of-view necessary for theatre."[7]

If Thérèse Raquin looks forward to a "theatre of everyday life" in the 'experimental' ways in which it attempts to be real, or more fantastically, and to our virtual world, where, according to Jean Baudrillard and others (Situationists) spectacle and reality have merged—its use of traditional dramatic conventions and theatrical motifs (for instance, melodrama), meant by Zola to palliate his audience, also seem to leave some very substantial segments of the wall or window separating public from stage intact. Traditional elements abound in this middle-or-lower class drama; the play being essentially about lovers who murder so they can be together, and then are haunted and hounded to death by the ghost of their guilt, Macbeth is clearly in evidence, almost to the point of parody. The work is just as clearly an updated version of a late-medieval morality play, of sin and punishment by conscience, modernized by way of the psychology of guilt—though of course modern (secular) in the sense that there is no redemption, the crime and punishment being totally earthly. The play opens, in fact, very ominously, with an activity that seems far from the ordinary dominos and daily soup: the lover is painting a portrait of the husband he will murder, in the presence of the latter's mother and wife (already his mistress)! This painting, later hanging in their bedroom, will come alive, after the crime, when the lovers have married, where they will feel terrifyingly observed by it. Incredible also, if not exactly beyond belief, then extraordinary, is the spectacularly gloomy motif of the mother, who had become paralyzed by a stroke after she learned that her son had been murdered, sitting in a chair in the same room with the perpetrators, unable to make a sound or a sign to brand them as such, except with her angry eyes; then suddenly, waking out of her paralysis to accuse them of the crime, hounding them to the suicide with which the play ends!

Therefore, in some very essential ways, whatever the ambitions of Zola to revolutionize the theatre, by injecting elements of the ordinary, the stage here is still window on an other world that the audience cannot really regard as its own, otherwise it would be intolerable and abhorrent, in the way that we (most of us) turn away from examples of human misery and suffering that so abound, unfortunately, in the world around us; and this other world remains distinct and separate from the real world of the audience. It would seem also that the index of horror is, if anything, greater than that of *Macbeth*, to which it invites comparison, because the murderers in Zola's play, contrary to Shakespeare's, are so driven by their lusts and aggressive instincts there is no sense they had any choice in their deed, except, pathetically, retroactively, when there is a bit of tragic recognition. It would be then the very horror that would create the necessity for maintaining the separation between stage and public. The guarantees of verisimilitude Zola supplies (the ordinary activities etc.) make us believe that this is someone's reality; but the intensity, melodrama and hallucinatory quality of the horror mean that this can't possibly be our reality.[8] Reality and artificiality thus guarantee each other in their mutual authenticity, each sure that they are not the other and they can relate to each other only on that basis, or not at all.

An effect achieved by Zola, whether aimed at or not, or consistent with the reality he said he was trying to create for the stage with his naturalistic theatre, was doubtless the one Aristotle is supposed to have recommended as the purpose of tragedy—namely the famous *purgation*, or *catharsis*. The public, after the play, returns to its everyday life, cleansed of its unconscious fears and terrors, which they had seen brought to the surface, enacted, acted out, resolved and so left behind. Also distancing the stage of *Thérèse Raquin* from its audience is the fact that Zola's theatre here, as does his art in general, presents characters, if not from a distinctly lower social class than that of its public, then dramatically closer to enacting their 'lower' drives, in the sense of these being people who proceed to act on their desires, with minimal or seemingly nonexistent interference (before the act, at least) from conscience or superego mechanisms. This involves the unsentimental depiction of human beings (necessarily) unmotivated by altruistic considerations, and seemingly acting solely out of instinctual longings and

animal cravings.  If distance in traditional theatre was created by the fact that
the characters were much higher in social rank than the public, so behaving
more 'nobly' (or ignobly, as the case might be), here the distance is created
by the very lowness of the species here depicted: the human beast (as in
Zola's novel, *La Bête Humaine*, of 1890), some transitional form in the
devolution of human to animal, and missing(?) link between the realms
Naturalism so liked to join.   Here I think we need to reflect not only on the
future of theatre (and civilization) but also where it (we) came from most
remotely but not least relevantly: sacrifice, as in of the (scape) goat middle
syllable in Tra-Ged-Y[9], the one that culminated (maybe not) in the Cross.
They died for our desires, Nemesis collecting the debt they incurred for our
sakes.  The members of this lower class or sub-species "act like animals", so
we can continue to see ourselves as human beings.

Such a vicarious system, here qualified by the sheer poetry, complexity
and ambiguity of the horror which Zola's genius conveys is more blatant in
another play, one by another author, but which relates, if tangentially, the
naturalistic message: Charles Reade's adaptation, *Drink* (1879) from Zola's
novel, *L'Assomoir* (1877).[10]  The characters in this play are no longer even
remotely middle-class, as we might imagine those of *Thérèse Raquin*, but
patently proletarian, or even lumpen-proletarian, not only in behavior but
also in social standing.  It is difficult to imagine any member of such a cast
as part of a theatre-going public.  The stage is separated from the audience
much as might be a cage in a zoo—where the animals on display appeal to
curiosity, certainly not to empathy.  Such an audience is told of the evil that
alcohol causes in the lower orders of society, but is, if anything, reassured in
its own convivial habits: "Yes, mademoiselle, sensible, educated people like
you, can be temperate.  But experience proves that a poor workman is not
safe unless he abstain altogether."[11]  The drama is supposed to be about "real
life" of course, but this is someone else's "real life"; or *real* the way a prison,
slum, asylum, or hospital ward is; and so the domains of stage and audience
remain more or less comfortably separate.  Just as it is the nobility of the
characters that creates distance in traditional theatre, here it is their very
baseness that has the same effect.  The stage is still the window on a world
the public ultimately applauds for what it is and leaves behind: whether a
higher one it can't stay in, or the lower one it doesn't want to admit to—as
above, so below.

# II.   The Return of the Repressed: *Ghosts*

With Henrik Ibsen's *Ghosts* (1881) the situation of the theatergoer is far more ambiguous than it was for *Thérèse Raquin*.   Whatever the (stated) ambitions of Zola to break down the separations between stage and reality, these remain very solidly in place, owing to the very 'theatrical', even melodramatic nature of the compromises, if that is what they were, the author made between the experimental naturalism of his art and how much originality he thought his public was able to tolerate, or, intentions aside, he was practically capable of.[1]  Ibsen's play, on the other hand, is not a place where such 'compromises' abound, accounting doubtless for the raucous reception of the play when it was first staged.[2]

In the 'war' between Idealism and Realism, as recounted, for instance in Toril Moi's impassioned and wonderfully wide ranging (into painting and other arts than theatrical, as well as politics and cultural history), *Henrik Ibsen and the Birth of Modernism*, ending in a conclusive victory for Realism, that raged throughout the 19th century, Ibsen was no innocent bystander, and surely had much to do with its triumph. His enthusiastic response to the "naturalist manifesto" (Moi, p. 85) his friend and intellectual mentor George Brandes produced by way of his lectures, *Émigré Literature*, published in 1872, as well as his decision, from about the mid 1870's on, starting with *Pillars of Society*, to set all his plays contemporaneously, show us clearly where his sympathies lay. Yet Ibsen, maybe because he is too much a man of the theatre and it is just too engrained in him to see things from different perspectives and "speak with different voices", however would be unwilling, or even incapable of writing in conformity with any program, or for very long, even his own (unlike Zola, not that there isn't much more to Zola than 'experimental' naturalism, certainly in the novels!).

Nevertheless, that work of his where his naturalism is the purest and most uncompromising is surely *Ghosts*, and this quality doubtless made for its hostile, even hateful reception.   At a time when Ibsen was already a celebrated poet and dramatist, and starting to be even world-famous, "The theatres...hermetically sealed their doors, both in Scandinavia and Germany,

not daring to offer their public such fare.  The play's first performance—
strangely enough—took place in Chicago in 1882..." as Heiberg (p.218) tells
it, citing also the author's Cassandra of a warning in letter to his publisher:
" '*Ghosts* will perhaps cause alarm in certain circles, but that cannot be
helped.  If it did not, then it would not have been necessary to write it.' "
(216).

Yet only a few years later, with *The Wild Duck* (1884), where we still
find naturalism amply and maybe essentially, we can't help but notice that so
very much else is going on; for instance with that proto-surrealist (or is it
dada or absurdist?) fantasy of a forest where Old Ekdal keeps up his hunting
and tracking skills and his rifle booming.  There the pathetic younger teen,
soon-to-be-suicided Hedvig cares for the wounded bird that can no longer
fly, subject of the sermonizing allegorizing of Gregor Werle's stories of
creatures that get tangled up at·the bottom of the sea, to drown there for lack
of air.  There is clearly a heavy dose of Symbolism working on us here, in
*The Wild Duck*, adumbrating surely the theatre and poetry of such as
Schwob, Maeterlinck and Ghelderode, even a certain Synge (as we'll see
soon) as well as the later Ibsen (*Little Eylof, Lady from the Sea,
Rosmersholm,* and that 'last will and testament' of an epilogue, *When We
Dead Awaken*), who will take it so much further.

Paradoxically, that very *honesty* which *Ghosts* so blatantly recommends,
by dramatizing the hidden costs of bourgeois, desire-denying, disease-
causing (through frustration) hypocrisy, turns out to be the *villain* of *The
Wild Duck*, since it  is Gregor Werle's maniacal acting-out of a project to
establish 'total honesty' in Hjalmar and Gina's marriage which precipitates
the catastrophe.  Honesty, in a vertiginous transformation has switched sides
from the Real to the Ideal; the Real has become the new Ideal; so at least
here, the new enemy: White is the New Black, Honesty the New Dishonesty!

This makes retroactively the naturalism of *Ghosts* something of an
experiment to the second degree, since naturalism is already an experiment,
one with 'scientific' pretensions, on the effect of context (society, culture,
environment, heredity) on humans and human behavior, an experiment (on
his public, himself too, doubtless), Ibsen found it necessary to undertake no
more than once.  Everywhere else in Ibsen there is something *else* working:
Whether the Utopian or Dystopian quality of the hopes and indictments
conveyed or implied in the feminism of such women-centered plays as *Doll's
House, Hedda Gabler,* and certainly *Lady from the Sea* (where you have that
rare example, maybe unique, in Ibsen, of a husband actually allowing his
wife to choose whether or not she wants to stay with him, granting her a
freedom and dignity the women in his other plays are denied...); or the
pejorative, over-determined  analyses of the damaging machismo and
megalomania of even (or especially) the well-meaning male hero in *Pillars
of Society, Enemy of the People, The Master Builder,  John Gabriel
Borkman*; or the mystical moments more than hinted at—the Symbolist

elements—there's always some other place we can emerge, at least in imagination, than facing a blank wall of destruction and condemnation (to frustration and disease, or at best, survival by way of hypocrisy and lies) by the mere dint of circumstance, we come up against in *Ghosts*. Here we find ourselves where the free will is minimal, the determinacy and therefore naturalism is as naked, pure and undiluted as we're ever going to get it, at least in Ibsen.

Here in *Ghosts*, as opposed to Zola's *Thérèse Raquin*, there is no murder, pictures don't come alive, where the ghosts are not those of the unjustly dead demanding the interventions of Nemesis. *Ghosts* shocks and unsettles instead by way of uncovering and reveling: by lifting the lid from the pressure cooker of middle-class respectability and hypocrisy, forcing its public into the snake pit of thwarted desire and, especially sexual repression and frustration. "Sooner murder an infant in its cradle than nurse unacted desires" and "He who desires but acts not, breeds pestilence" are Blake maxims that could well be posted over the threshold to the hell of this kind of world.

Ibsen is aiming the arrow of a truth that hurts-in-order-to-heal at an audience that cannot move from the bulls eye of (being) its target; for, unquestionably, Ibsen's characters, though fully realized as existential beings and personalities, depend for the absolutely compelling dramatic sense they make on the fact that they are also types. By failing themselves they have failed each other and humanity, in the sense of the Kantian imperative that by acting (or not) we accord our approval to others to do likewise. The Alvings' mockery of a marriage is surely meant to represent the travesty of that repressive institution in the Western World. Their blasted lives, whether their own, or their son's, a victim of hereditary syphilis, and that of Captain Alving's illegitimate daughter, raised as a servant without knowing who she was and destined for a life of prostitution—these are equally meant to designate the ineluctable outcome of the sins (of hypocrisy and cowardice) of the parents. Meddlesome, noxious and really dangerous, the parish pastor, Manders, is doubtless meant not only as an indictment of himself as an individual but clearly also as a statement that religion constitutes a social malignancy, certainly harmful, possibly fatal, and unquestionably degrading. Engstrand, likewise, the unscrupulous carpenter who married the servant who was Alving's mistress, partaking in the remunerated charade of pretending to be the father of his 'daughter' is clearly, as well as a brilliantly individualized dramatic creation, foiling, in his comically cynical materialism, the sentimental seriousness of the main characters. Engstrand is the very type of the working man who cannot afford the niceties of middle-class 'honor'.[3]

Since its characters tend also to be types who cling tightly to outward appearances (or in the case of Engstrand, who exploits this quality in his 'betters'), preferring hypocrisy, for example, to blatant criminality or rebellion, it seems a safe assumption that an audience is much more likely to recognize itself, however unflattering that might be, in *Ghosts* than in *Thérèse Raquin*. In this sense Ibsen has moved along further than Zola was willing or capable of—in the direction of narrowing the distance between stage and public, theatre and reality. Nevertheless, the two domains of actor and audience still remain, in Ibsen, *distinct*, if porous and fluid, because of the construction of the action of the play around moments of heightened intensity. The play, in fact, starts off on the eve of the opening of the Orphanage that is supposed to consecrate the memory of the deceased Captain Alving. Coincidentally?, it is also the very time of his son's unhappy return, prompted by unmistakable symptoms of the hereditary syphilis that will make it impossible to 'have a life' (continue to paint) or eventually to (want to) live at all. Theatrical also is the fact that the son's final breakdown occurs onstage, as the end and culmination of the dramatic action; an event whose advent has triggered the revelation of the realities of disease, promiscuity, hypocrisy and suffering that were hiding behind the facade of middle class respectability, as they do and must, of course, it's more than implied, for all of us!

After the curtain has fallen on the night of an Oswald who has gone blind in front of its very eyes, and the audience has applauded (and/or squirmed or fumed, as its first 'puritan' critics apparently did), it returns to its daily life, putting this night behind it, as it must; for there is then an ambiance of an intolerable "horror of it all"[4] generated by this play, especially at its almost un-watchable conclusion, the ultimate in conceivable heartbreak of a son asking his mother to help him take his own life. This is a denouement that will fascinate, of course, but will also push the dramatic action towards the ultimately 'taboo' space of sacrifice, tragedy and purgation, the way we have described it functioning, even partially at least defeating the intentions of creating a naturalistic theater that joins stage and reality, also for Zola in *Thérèse Raquin*.

# III.  The Nature of the Beast: *The Power of Darkness*

In *The Power of Darkness* (1887, but, because of censorship, not performed, in Russia, until 1895[1]), we find Tolstoy, as pervasively in his work, intent on breaking down the separations between life and art.  Of course what Tolstoy considered life by then had a lot to do with his Christian agenda.  In fact, "The period of the 1880's was one in which, on principle, Tolstoy had renounced literary activity in favor of spiritual and educational products"[2]; so Tolstoy likely allowed himself to be lured back into literature by the prospect of using the reality-effect of recently created naturalistic theatre to teach a vivid moral lesson about the opprobrium of a life-without-God and the corresponding blessedness of one with.  Ironically, in Tolstoy's hands, theatrical naturalism represents 'the human animal' in terms of a sheer brutality that neither Zola nor Ibsen come anywhere near: a man writhing in pain on stage from the effects of a poison administered by his wife; a 'dead' baby that turns out to be alive, thrown around the stage like a hot potato, then just about smothered in front of us by its own father etc.; just as if one needed a religious pretext to bypass the taboos that were keeping us from realizing Zola's goal of separating stage from real life.  In this sense the religious Tolstoy is more of a forerunner of Tennessee Williams than the secular Zola and Ibsen.

  *The Power of Darkness* is a play about "sin and redemption" among the Russian peasantry, based on an actual court case, of 1880, with which Tolstoy was acquainted, involving adultery, murder, infanticide and confession.  Adultery and infanticide among the peasantry had also been the subject of a prior play, which Tolstoy knew well, *Bitter Fate* (1859), by Alexei Pisemsky; a likely literary influence was also Dostoevsky's great novel *Crime and Punishment* (1866), for the theme of the corrosive effect of guilt on the mind of a murderer.

  As the play opens, a rich peasant (Pyotr, age 42) has been taken ill, while his second wife (Anisya, age 32), who has taken up with an attractive laborer

(Nikita, age 25, who seems to "fuck everything in sight"), is waiting for him to die, and also keeping an eye peeled for where he has hidden his money. This Realm of Darkness is clearly a place where matter only matters. The laborer, as well as being the wife's lover, has also been involved with an orphan girl (Marina, age 22), whom he abandons to her fate after she has become pregnant by him. Encouraged by Nikita's greedy and rapacious mother, Matryona, Anisya starts poisoning her husband by adding certain toxic powders to his tea, while intensifying her efforts to find and seize the hidden money before others can get their hands on it. In sheer horror Tolstoy outdoes Zola, who had presented the husband's drowning in *Thérèse Raquin* as reported action, and of course, Ibsen, in *Ghosts*, where the sins are more failures in heart and nerve than actual crimes. So we are shown Nikita bluntly 'dumping' Marina, who's desperately in love with him (Act I, sc. 19); which seems polite in comparison to the devastating scenes 9-14 of the following act, in which Pyotr is shown twisting in pain, and practically dying on stage, under the effect of the poisons his wife has given him with his tea. Taking advantage of an opportunity afforded her when he was leaning on her in his agony and escorting him offstage to his deathbed, we are told that Matryona (Nikita's sharpeyed mother), had discovered the money tied in a bag around the dying man's neck, under his nightshirt. The money, after being ripped off the dying (or dead) man's body by his wife, Anisya, winds up, through the manipulations of Matryona, in possession of everyone's lover, her son, Nikita! As was the case for the guilty lovers of *Thérèse Raquin*, the marriage that then follows is also the death of love, or at least romance.

Nikita then starts an affair with Pyotr's daughter, Akulina (age 16, "hard of hearing and simple minded"), by a previous wife—she then becomes pregnant, giving birth to the embarrassing child secretly, shortly before she is to be married off to an unsuspecting neighbor. The stage is then set for what may well be the most disgusting scene in theatre since the "out vile jelly" with which the loyal Gloucester paid with his eyes for his loyalty to Lear, before he was told to "smell his way to Dover"—the interminably painful, carefully detailed, exactly described infanticide of Act IV, scenes 10-16, performed in about as brutally real a manner as is possible without actually crushing a live baby to death in front of our eyes. Scene 10 discovers Nikita meditating or thinking out loud of refusing to go along with the women (his mother and wife), who he knows are planning to murder the baby. There follows two nasty persuasion scenes—right out of *Richard III*,[3] where the women get him to oblige. First it's his mother, Matryona's turn, who enters holding a lugubrious lantern and shovel (sc. 11), to be joined by the wife, in the next scene, so he hears it from all sides, at the end of which he yields to their entreaties, disappearing down a doorway to the cellar, leaving the door open, so that we can hear him scraping away, then finally calling up for the baby to be brought down to him (sc. 14). Matryona thoughtfully inquires if

Anisya has remembered to put a cross on the baby (after all, it's her grandchild); Anisya complains how difficult it was ripping cross and/or baby from the mother's arms, wanting Nikita to take it from her hands, whereas he insists she bring it down by herself. Whereupon she *throws* the baby at him, which Nikita, along with the audience, of course, then realizes is *alive*, even though he had been told it was already dead:

> NIKITA
>     (*catches it*): It's alive! Oh, my God, it's movin' It's alive! What am I gonna...
> ANISYA
>     (snatches the baby out of his arms and throws it into the cellar): Choke it quick and it won't be alive." [66][4]

Mercifully we don't actually witness the execution, but only hear a play-by-play live action account of Nikita's covering it with a board, which he sits on, thereby crushing it to death: "An' how its little bones crunched under me. Crr... Crr.." [67], he whimpers to his mother, leaving not much to the imagination, what with sound effects. Essentially the rest of the play follows through, complete with some of Nikita's grisly flashbacks on the "crunching of the bones", on the paradigm of the 'guilty conscience' of, say, *Macbeth*, which, as we have seen, in Zola's 'naturalization' of it for *Thérèse Raquin*, serves as a modern psychological equivalent of the classical nemesis that pursues and destroys the evildoer—with the distinction, that for Tolstoy, as for Dostoevsky, we would be dealing, whether we like it or not, with the voice of God.

Except possibly for this religious element, this is programmatic naturalism at work here: men and women, at least those that define and create the action, portrayed as subject to and victim of their animal cravings, proceeding directly from wish to satisfaction by way of every crime in the book! Naturalism's fondness for denizens of the lower depths and lower classes is well in evidence here too, since the lives such strata are obliged to lead are more clearly the result of a combination of environment and heredity than those of higher classes who can hide more easily the facts of their determination behind the veil of the myth of freedom. However, assuming, safely, that the public is middle class or above, there is also a distancing effect at work here, with the stage becoming a window into a world not its public's own, or not for long, either of a slumming kind of exoticism, and/or a representation of the timeless rite of the sacrifice that drama, especially tragedy likes to repeat.

However, a play about the lower classes does not cease to be elitist simply because of its cast of characters; Nikita's ultimate confession, even though it comes from a peasant, arose from a situation of positively Kierkegaardian anguish and complexity. Although the author obviously is thinking of himself here as engaged in a work of reeducation, showing his public the error of its ways and the path through darkness toward redemption, the performance record of such models seems more to show that for most of that humanity Tolstoy was trying to enlighten, such behavior would be more of an unattainable absolute, fit only for those who can 'afford' such honesty,[5] or some very special individuals, maybe like the author himself, or an actor in a play.

# IV. The Dialectic of the Master and the Slave: *Miss Julie*

August Strindberg, with *Miss Julie* (1888) is working on a deeper, if not a 'higher', level than Tolstoy, that of the unconscious mental processes. Strindberg adds an element that was largely absent even in the psychological theatre of Ibsen and Zola, that of childhood:[1]  In *Miss Julie* the two protagonists, Miss Julie, the "boss's daughter" and Jean, the valet who seduces her (and/or is seduced by her) are very much the disturbed children they once were—Miss Julie is still the unwanted child, dragged unwillingly into a power struggle between her parents and the world and each other, therefore not equipped for any kind of autonomy, as she confides to Jean:

> I came into the world against my mother's wishes, as far as I can understand.  She wanted to bring me up as a child of nature, and what's more, to learn everything a boy had to learn, so that I might be an example of how a woman can be as good as a man. [85];

while Jean is the *Son of a Servant* (title of a Strindberg novel), to whom the shit of the ruling classes is the divinest perfume:

> I sneaked in, I saw, and marveled.... There I caught sight of a pink dress and a pair of white stockings, it was you.  I crawled under a pile of weeds and I mean under— under thistles that pricked me and wet dirt that stank." [74].

When "push comes to shove" really it is the subconscious that supplies the energy: no matter how bold of a game he talks, one ring of the bell and Jean will be ready with the father's shined boots; while Julie accepts Jean's self-serving advice to commit suicide just as a child would whose decisions are made by others "who know what's best for it."

The author, at this point in his life at least,[2] owes no allegeance to any transcendent religious or mystical idea or ideal, of the sort that inhabits *The Power of Darkness*.  A kitchen, which is the setting of the play, is ideal for emphasizing the influence of primary biological processes and appetites, a real focus here, as for naturalism in general.

A curious twist, this love affair, or, brutally put, one-night stand between a master (mistress!), and a servant on Hegel's famous Master-Slave Dialectic of the *Phenomenology* (1807), whereby it is the master's willingness to die that demarcates him from the slave's acceptance of any degradation or compromise, for the sake of living, or to name it more aptly, survival... For Karl Marx and the war between the classes, of which the individual is a mere avatar, not to mention Schopenhauer and his irresistible Will, Darwin and the compelling Survival of the Fittest, as well as some very relevant others, like Kierkegaard, Nietzsche and Bachofen (feminism and matriarchy, Strindberg's bête noire) have come between Hegel and *Miss Julie*. For example, does the Master still rule if she (!), in Schopenhauerian resignation, or obscurely but surely obeying some compelling proto-Freudian death-drive, commits suicide, furthermore at the behest and for the convenience of her antagonist in a struggle between the sexes and classes—that she is losing?

To register the consequences of this intellectual and cultural evolution or devolution, we find here Strindberg taking full advantage of the recent creation of a naturalistic theatre that had challenged, in so many ways, the distinctions, hierarchies and separations of the traditional stage in relation to its audience. Just as Hegel's Master and Slave have become much more ambiguous, fluid and nugatory categories, so the Stage has merged with the rhythms, opportunities (or what seem like such in an age when traditions are weakening) and decor of real life. Fittingly, since the catastrophe(s) that visit, sooner or later, the chanciest of us don't necessarily observe the decorum of the five-act formula, nor behave according to the rules of Aristotelian tragedy or conform to the inevitably Shakespearian dénouement of an order and orderliness that is restored after it has been traumatically, but only temporarily, violated—this is a one-acter, and one that strikes with the inevitability and belatedness (to do anything about it) of a bolt of lightning.

In our modern world, where fate and design have faded, or survived only as variously effective exotic or esoteric resorts, it is chance that is king. Moreover since it is in the everyday, the ordinary that we are most open, liable and vulnerable, here there is a minimum of stage scenery and formality, in this play that can appropriately be staged in a coffee-shop[3] or some other intimate or even 'private' space, with its audience sitting practically in the kitchen with the actors, so close up to the action they are virtually participating in it.

To keep the play from drifting into the category of a documentary or case-history, which I think Tolstoy's *Power of Darkness*, based, pretty closely apparently, on an actual court case, flirts with, a certain minimum dramatic distance is maintained by the extreme compression and poetic intensity of the play, reinforced by the placing of the action in the "otherworldly" time of Midsummer Night's Eve in this Scandinavian Land of the Midnight Sun; as well as by a sprinkling of the salt of an ominous symbolism—for instance Julie's riding whip, which she used to make her ex-lover jump over, or her beloved bird, which Jean unceremoniously kills, as too much trouble to take along with them on their projected elopement. However these more conventional or traditional elements serve more as breathers or relief from a too-abrupt (to tolerate) shock of recognition of a Brave New World where naked power rules: In the end, inescapable is the realization that Julie has been put to death, like multitudes of others, by the cruelties of nature and society; in other words, at least as far as the victims are concerned, at the moment of their immolation, by the sheer absurd and meaningless workings of blind chance. An audience is thereby presented with a new world of power, in which the social classes are in a state of violent perturbation and equilibrium and in which, naturally, no one's place will be sure. It is as if Strindberg is depicting, with the prophetic vision of an artist, and experimentally[4], momentous changes which are bound to engulf everybody, or have already—as they have the all-too-(in)human characters the players here represent.

# V. The War Between the Classes: *The Weavers*

With Gerhart Hauptmann's *The Weavers* (1892), there is a qualitative break in the evolution of a Naturalistic Theatre toward a merging of stage and public we have been following. Here it is a matter of the resolute turning of theatre toward the external world, of which it purports to be a faithful, if partisan reflection. Strangely but truly, fifty years before the play was written, Act I of *The Weavers* was described, and in exact detail, by Frederick Engels, commenting a popular realistic painting of the time, called "Weavers Delivering the Finished Cloth", by K. Hübner :

> It represents some Silesian weavers bringing linen cloth to the manufacturer, and contrasts very strikingly cold–hearted wealth on one side, and despairing poverty on the other. The well-fed manufacturer is represented with a face as red and unfeeling as brass, rejecting a piece of cloth which belongs to a woman; the woman, seeing no chance of selling the cloth, is sinking down and fainting, surrounded by her two little children, and hardly kept up by an old man; a clerk is looking over a piece, the owners of which are with painful anxiety waiting for the result; a young man shows to his desponding mother the scanty wages he has received for his labor; an old man, a girl, and a boy, are sitting on a stone bench and waiting for their turn; and two men, each with a piece of rejected cloth on his back, are just leaving the room, one of whom is clenching his fist in rage, whilst the other, putting his hand on his neighbor's arm, points up to heaven, as if saying: be quiet, there is a judge to punish him. This whole scene is going on in a cold and unhomely-looking lobby, with a stone floor: only the manufacturer stands upon a piece of carpeting; whilst on the other side of the painting, behind a bar, a view is opened into a luxuriously furnished counting-house, with splendid curtains and looking-glasses, where some clerks are writing, undisturbed by what is passing behind them...[1]

Quite as exactly Engels had described in an earlier text the rest of the play that would be produced so effectively 50 years later—the Weavers responding to their oppression through revolutionary violence, involving destruction of the property of owners, including machinery, as well as fighting a pitched battle with the military, one which they at first won.[2] One cannot imagine what they both considered this exemplary proletarian event not coming up in conversation between Marx and Engels, when they first met in Paris in August of 1844, for early in that month the former had described the Weavers Revolt, in a radical German language newspaper then being published in Paris, in absolutely glowing terms. Marx, even at the time, elsewhere singled out for special praise the effectiveness and intelligence of the Weavers Song, which was also to become later a compelling *leitmotif* in Hauptmann's play, for the sophisticated proletarian consciousness there manifested, thereby dispelling the myths of working class ignorance and helplessness being disseminated by the bourgeoisie, through their apologists (Bauer and the Young Hegelian Company). The Weavers were, accordingly, on the cutting edge of the proletarian revolution, in advance, in some significant ways, of their French and English counterparts:

> First of all, recall the *song of the weavers*[3] that bold *call* to struggle, in which there is not even a mention of hearth and home, factory or district, but in which the proletariat at once, in a striking, sharp, unrestrained and powerful manner, proclaims its opposition to the society of private property.[4] The Silesian uprising *begins* precisely with what the French and English workers' uprisings *end*, with consciousness of the nature of the proletariat. The action itself bears the stamp of this *superior* character. Not only machines, these rivals of the workers are destroyed, but also *ledgers*, the titles to property...[5]

Stage and reality are closer here than they have ever been in the history of theater, at least since the Renaissance, when our represented reality starting becoming a secular one, and certainly in its naturalistic avatar. However credible or incredible the characters have been that we have been describing in previous plays, there is no question that they are fictional creations, therefore allowing its public a certain minimal distance from them; but how, indeed, is an audience, especially a class-conscious one—which it must be in Paris of 1890, a century after the French Revolution, not to mention a half-century of Proudhon, Marx and Engels (and the quashed revolution of 1848), Blanqui, 20 years after the Commune—to feel itself distinct from the revolutionary events depicted on this stage, for whom its reality has been, and continues to be, shaped by these events? Always before, even in historical drama, for instance in Shakespeare, Corneille, Schiller and Hugo, the characters, however class-defined, are first-and-foremost individuals. Here, with *The Weavers*, the characters are first of all representatives of their class and only secondarily individuals.[6]

After the compelling and heart-wrenching pageant of the workers misery, with its concomitant images of ruling-class hypocrisy, callousness and greediness, how not cheer on the weavers in their violent assault on the system that oppresses them and those who profit from it? As an analyst-dramatist of the Weavers Revolt, Hauptmann will allow for more complexity and nuance, of course, than the polemics, however brilliant and righteous of Marx and Engels—for instance, making room, on the workers' side, for the probability, maybe even the (limited) validity of a religious response to exploitation—that is resignation to it as the price of a future place in heaven. Interestingly this is the only alternative to proletarian violence that Hauptmann will honor with any significant stage time,[7] in the presence of the aged weaver, Old Hilse who rejects as demonic any recourse to violence; it is significant, too that he dies, ironically, and perhaps as a negative model, at the end of the play, victim of a soldier's bullet, from which he has refused to take cover.

The public of such a production must be seen as half-way participating in a demonstration, either as sitting on the edge of its seats, ready to join whatever would be the current equivalent (surely not in short supply!) of the Weavers Revolt, or, in case of a regrettable but unavoidable identification with the propertied, squirming in them... For this is legitimate, understandable, productive and tonic revolutionary violence being demonstrated here, sanctioned by history and the most prestigious and persuasive names in Communist Theory, Marx and Engels, then subject of a very sympathetic, expertly crafted and very successful production of André Antoine's Théâtre Libre, becoming thereby the cutting-edge of both politics and modernist aesthetics. These insurrectionary events thereby were justified. They called for imitation, the way Eisentstein's film *Battleship Potemkin* (1925) was to function later, to justify and continue the Revolution of 1917.

Any distance at all here is unlikely, since class struggle, which is the play's theme, albeit set during the famous revolt of the Silesian Weavers of June 2-4, 1844, is still very much in evidence in Europe of the 1890's, about halfway between the Paris Commune of 1870 and the Bolshevik Revolution of 1917. Even a half-a-century later, to dramatize the Weavers Revolt, and to present that production as the major theatrical event of the Théâtre Libre, in Paris, in 1892, with the events of the Commune, of 1870 still very much of a living memory and example, must have seemed far from innocent. For this is quintessentially, *political* theatre we are dealing with here. In the careers of Karl Marx and Friedrich Engels, who had just met and 'joined forces' in Paris, in August of 1844, the Weavers Revolt, which had just occurred a few months before, and whose impact on the political situation in Germany (and so Europe) they still deemed seminal and catalytic,[8] occupies, in fact, a threshold position. It demonstrated and embodied both the legitimacy and the effectiveness of proletarian violence against their exploiters and their expropriation of the ruling class. Thereby it helped wean Communism away from the abstract humanism and humanitarianism of such as Feuerbach and Proudhon, as well as responding to the scorn of some newly-conservative Young Hegelians, such as the Bauer brothers, for any role for the working class on the world-historical stage—impelling it directly on the main road toward the Revolution(s) of 1848 and the 'battle' ideology of the Communist Manifesto that was to become its Declaration of Independence. Two cardinal works from the 1844-45 period of their nascent collaboration reflect this signal turning of Marx and Engels toward the predicament of the working class and its capacity to do something about it: *The Condition of the Working Class in England* by the latter and *The Holy Family or Critique of Critical Criticism*, signed by both.[9] A central statement of *The Holy Family* would equally apply to the mood and message of Hauptmann's later *Weavers*:

> Since the conditions of life of the proletariat sums up all the conditions of life of society today in their most inhuman form...it follows that the proletariat can and must emancipate itself. (Marx and Engels, Vol.4, pp. 36-37).

Artistic and political emancipation here coincide; for just as the Weavers Revolt marks the independence of the proletariat from the tutelage and initiative of the Bourgeoisie, so *The Weavers*, "high-water mark" and really the culmination of that Naturalistic theatre that was inspired by Zola and so effectively espoused by André Antoine[10], marks the independence of the Stage from the tutelage and tyranny of dramatic convention; from then on it is no longer necessary, sometimes not even advisable to invent anything. Increasingly theatre is inspired by crimes and court cases. History or reality is theatre enough—if the events represented are only significant enough in their impact that they practically pour off the frame and framework of the stage into the swift currents of daily life there where the struggle for food, dignity, solidarity is an ever renewed challenge.

This is a Faustian world, where no moment is asked to "stay", a Nietzschean one, of "the transvaluation of all values" (Morse Peckham's phrase for it), where yesterday's or today's good is not tomorrow's, where the only peace is the one between battles. Here there is no moment of seeming glory or peace that doesn't immediately slip into hubris and danger; and likewise no abject misery and humiliation that doesn't slide into a countermovement of overcoming. This is a world truly and disturbingly like our own, in the very process of mutation, where the lessons we learn so painfully yield to the ever more painful lesson of forgetting them, one in the throes of the pitiless struggle for survival between the classes that compose it, as well as conflict within classes for domination. Audience sympathy, though obviously meant to lean toward the "downtrodden", is not necessarily limited to that class—as this sympathy is qualified by irrational and destructive elements (who, in the play, drink up the wine cellar of the looted manufacturer) in the "army of the proletariat", as well as by a sobering realization of the obvious subjection of the owning class to a vicious competitive market, over which they have no control.[11] Here dramatic presentation, historical fact and Marxist interpretation, and the turbulent social and political, not to mention aesthetic context, in which the play was written and staged—all of this fuses into a complex new reality. Any division between stage and public, of the sort Zola and his acolytes said they wanted to dissolve, has been if not (momentarily) abrogated, then very seriously challenged, for this is a play that positively dares its public to go on with life as usual, or even to go on believing or 'acting' as if there is such a thing. The stage here merely incarnates conflicts that are rife in the society at large; it does not, as theater traditionally had to do, in order to continue to be what people considered such, resolve things. Shakespeare's, Corneille's, Racine's most tormented tragedies restore the orders they upset in their beginnings, or make convincing motions in that direction. Even in the tradition-challenging Naturalistic theatre we have been looking at there are motions of resolution to the bleakest of situations. In Zola, the guilty are punished, by themselves if not by others; the 'education' afforded by *Ghosts* will not be lost on its progeny, hopefully; the sparks of Tolstoy's Christian God catch fire in the heart of the evildoer; even the blackness of Miss Julie's night is relieved by the light that's appearing as she heads out of the kitchen to kill herself...

*The Weavers* is the first play that won't end, even unhappily. It just stops, the first of the No Exit chambers that have become the best places for Art to put us when it dares to tell us the truth, if there still is one, about Life. For Hauptmann does not resolve the conflicts, either between classes or even within the working class (for instance, between the apolitical religious and the insurrectionary secular elements), but arrests his drama before the final historical defeat of the Silesian weavers. He leaves his audience therefore dangling, free to believe in the tonic overall effect of the events on other revolutionary movements, as Marx and Engels described them, or to leave with some other attitude, amazed, despairing, frustrated—or maybe hoping, in what was to become the constructive Brechtian sense of a non-theatrical offstage reality to be mended. On this stage all is flux and movement, no victory can be final, no defeat decisive. The individual roles tend to dissolve into the urgency of a process that overwhelms the willing and the unwilling alike. Old Hilse may well play the (religious) conservative, but his action demonstrates the meaninglessness of his words, as he dies more than half-looking for the bullet that kills him:

VOICES
(*From the entrance hall.*) Get away from the window, Father Hilse!
OLD HILSE
Not me! Not if ya all go crazy. (*To* MOTHER HILSE *with mounting excitement.*) Here my Heavenly Father put me. Right, Mother? Here we'll stay sittin' and doin' what's our duty—even if the snow was to catch fire.
*He begins to weave. A volley is fired. Fatally hit,* OLD HILSE *rises from his stool and then falls forward over the loom.* [last scene of play]

P. Skrine, emphasizing the same unprecedented originality of the play remarked here, called *The Weavers*:

> the culmination of Naturalism's proletarian strand....The greatest Naturalist drama is one in which plot and hero are dispensed with altogether, and in which speech seems to emerge spontaneously from the characters themselves.[12]

Human speech itself, to mention another theatrical 'convention', in this context begins to seem like a sublime irrelevance, since the actions transpire on a deeper level than words can match, and also because people no longer speak as individuals but as representative of classes and interests:

> *At the same time loud cries of "Hurray" are heard. Shouting "Hurray" the people who have been standing in the entrance hall rush outside.* [ibid].

These directions to the actors here to rush outside can only mean to rush, symbolically at least, into or towards the street, there where all revolutions begin, while reminding the public, as Brecht would do later, of the challenges awaiting them. Here the author has moved towards transforming his audience, the public, all of us—into a population of players. Are not players a public too?

# VI.  In the Country of the Blind:
*The Lower Depths*

The environment, and the process which creates it, and/or can or cannot change it, had emerged as triumphant, in the sense of having the last 'word', with Hauptmann, and had swallowed up utterly the stage and its players with the socially cynical skits of Oscar Méténier.[1]  In Maxim Gorky's *The Lower Depths* (1902), the stage becomes a "real-life locality", an inn where characters—those "former people" that the oppressive system has one way or another deprived of the privileges of privacy, status and identity—live, love, work, gamble, drink, sicken, hope,  endlessly argue, die—in other words where the totality of their lives are on display.  Although the characters are variously motivated, depending on their situations (how 'hopeless' it is, in the sense of their ability to foster a fantasy of improvement), either to adjust to (there are "privileged" positions, such as landlord, even in a ghetto!) or to escape from this setting, everybody must relate to it *first of all*.  If the sixty-year-old pilgrim, Luka, brings a different point of view it is only because he has come from another place—and if his words seem strange and unreal, it is because they have not been born in *The Lower Depths*—that is, they were created for and by another environment and then applied externally to this one.  In an unfinished sketch for a film (never made) [Gorky, 153-59] of *The Lower Depths*, Gorky had described the "former life" of Luka; he had been a Village Chief who, taking advantage of his position, had seduced the wife of a poor peasant. After the peasant had committed suicide, in dramatic protest (in front of Luka's house; in his region it was customary to kill yourself in front of the dwelling of the one who wronged you), Luka became a repentant wanderer on the face of the earth.  In the play, however, Luka, is very much someone who comes from nowhere, disappearing just as mysteriously there.  His, then, is *The View from Nowhere*; no one else really comes to or leaves (except feet-first) from *The Lower Depths* in this No Exit universe of Gorky—which isn't really so true about Jean Renoir's masterly, if not terribly faithful film adaptation of the play, *Les Bas Fonds* (1936).  In the final scene of Renoir's film, the already hardened young (age 28) career criminal, Peppel, manages to elope (thereby escaping from *The Lower Depths* ) with the younger sister, Natasha (age 20) of the corrupt landlord's wife, with whom he had broken off an affair.    In the play, no such "Hollywood ending" happens; an elopement is planned, certainly, as the only thing that can save either of them (Peppel from a life of crime, Natasha from a marriage of convenience), but it doesn't come off—since after the landlord dies in the middle of a violent dispute with Peppel, the latter is accused of killing him with premeditation by none other than his 'fiancée' Natasha. He is then arrested and led off to jail, while Natasha is self-committed to some kind of hospital, presumably mental[2] —as if to say that the only way out of *The Lower Depths*, is even lower, into incarceration or institutionalization; as if poverty weren't jail enough!

Naturalism, which insists on placing everybody would place Luka in the place of  those who admit to no place, or who cannot (yet) be defined as belonging to one.  It's tempting, and probably makes some sense, too, to regard him as a persona of the writer, quintessentially the man-without-a-country, the exile and ñomad (James Joyce) of modern times.  Much earlier in his life Gorky too had wandered across Russia, a "pilgrim" like Luka, and a homeless vagabond.  Corresponding to the hopeful fantasies, stories and reassurances of Luka would be the Prospero's magic wand of a pen of Gorky; and making of the writer's position at once a necessary, as well as vulnerable one.  By making it possible for some to hope—for instance the dispossessed and disenfranchised of these lower depths, the writer, like Luka, is threatening the interests of others: the ruling classes, here represented by the proprietors of the inn, who, constantly asking to see Luka's either nonexistent or non-forthcoming passport, want either to 'nail him down' to a solid identity with which they can control, intimidate and tame him, or failing that, to get rid of him.  Significantly, among the vast cast of characters (a kind of cross-section of the 'has beens' and 'never was-es' of the population) in this play, it's only the landlord and the landlady who generate absolutely no sympathy on the part of Luka.  The exile the inn-owners eventually decree for Luka has also been the fate of the writer, regarded as a dangerous seducer since Plato exiled poets from his republic, and just like the writer (and artist in general, of course), indeed, since at least the end of patrimony, so Luka is cut off from all necessary connection to the economy: we still haven't answered Don Quixote's question to *his* innkeeper as to who is supposed to pay the knight-errant's rent! A dentist will be compensated by the tooth, but no writer can count on being paid by the page, nor artist by the canvas.  On the contrary, in order to 'do their best' writers and artists are often obliged to abstract themselves and their works from all consideration of remuneration, or even safety, braving not only poverty, but also political persecution and worse.

Let's not exaggerate the powers of art, however, as its 'enemies' and also some of its 'romantic' friends might be inclined, for there is a sense in which Luka, as 'writer', demonstrates the futility and limits of the word as vividly as he has its power. Fundamental modifications in politics, economy, morality, culture are not a matter of only discourse; blood, sweat and tears must be mixed in with the ink in this witches brew. It is alas too late or too early to save or change many, or maybe even very many, or for very long; and it will always be so, even if that in itself is no reason not to try to 'even the playing field', insofar as we are able—given the way the dice of life are loaded before we even get a chance to throw them, assuming we do.

It is true that Luka intervenes effectively in some ways: he helps the dying Anna with stories of heaven, encourages the prostitute Nastya in her comforting fantasy of a one true love that has been hers, which she has just culled from a romantic novel she has been reading (in this inn, reading is a public activity!); his most effective intervention is a timely cough he utters from under a table, from where, invisible, he has been listening to a violent altercation between Peppel, the thief lover, and Kostylyov, the cuckolded landlord. This keeps the latter from being murdered, temporarily, a benefit that seems to be only a postponement, or some kind of lucky chance, for Kostylyov dies later, however, during another brawl with Peppel, and, as a matter of fact, a whole innfull of lodgers. For, generally, in critical situations, when life and death are at stake Luka is as irrelevant as a preacher on the battlefield when the bullets start flying. He's as helpless to stop anything from happening as he is to make anything happen, so finally his words are more remarkable for their disconnection from and irrelevance to reality than for their impact and influence: He can't keep Anna from dying, Kostylyov from being killed; his support for Nastya's romantic fantasy doesn't abstract her from her prostitute's life. On the contrary it may have made it more tolerable. A big miss certainly is the story he tells the Actor about the nonexistent hospital where he can be cured, gratis, of his alcoholism, since when the Actor discovers the truth, there being no shortage of enlighteners at this inn of the disillusioned, he hangs himself: end of the play, period, and his life too, which he might have dragged on for a few more drunken years anyway... The seemingly excellent advice he gave to the adulterous landlady's younger sister, Natasha, who has been exploited by the owners as a domestic drudge, to run off with Peppel, the career thief who's fallen in love with her, and promises to 'reform', doesn't exactly fall on deaf ears, but nevertheless was impossible for the characters in Gorky's play to follow.[3]

Luka, almost to the point where he could be regarded as a recreation of the personified abstractions of medieval drama, traffics in *hope*. He would incarnate that *Principle of Hope* the Marxist philosopher, Gorky's later contemporary, Ernst Bloch, would soon find startling and encouraging evidence of in the history of mystical and religious dissidence—for instance, in the career of the protestant revolutionary, Thomas Münzer, and the events and tragedy (extirpation—see the gruesome account of it in 'the first English novel', Thomas Nashe's *The Unfortunate Traveler)* of the proto-communist (community of women and property) Münster Anabaptist rebellion, based on Münzer's teachings, of the early 16th century.

How the characters respond to Luka is plainly a function of how badly they need to believe this 'message'. Thus, Anna, whose early death by tuberculosis is the leitmotif and background, while setting the mood for much of the action of the first half of the play, bonds very tightly with him. Anna has been undergoing the *social death*, which is preliminary to and a concomitant of a physical one. The next-most-desperate character in the play is of course the alcoholic Actor. Whereas the agonizing Anna is regaled with tales about the joys of heaven, the ruined Actor is charmed by "castle in Spain" type visions of a hospital, in this world, albeit at some distance, where such conditions as his are treated sympathetically, effectively and free-of-charge... Oh, Luka can't remember the *exact* name of the town where it's located, but he's very sure it exists, as will be the Actor, until at least shortly before the end of the play.

Basically no one himself and coming from nowhere and going there, Luka can be whoever a character wants him to be and say whatever someone likes to hear. Those that are absolutely grounded in private property, or cannot see beyond it, preeminently the inn-owners, have, of course, no use for him; while the others' reception ranges from suspicion, through grudging respect all the way toward absolute adulation. The intellectual (or formerly so) Satin's attitude toward him starts out as respectfully ironic, but takes a turn toward admiration at the end of the play. The young prostitute Nastya, with her dreams of a perfect lover right out of a cheap romantic novel, would rather listen to Luka's loving encouragement than the Baron's "truth" (her pimp-lover, who lives off her, by her and his admission, "like a worm off an apple"):

BARON
    (Laughing.) Do you think this true, Grandpa? She took it all from the book *Fatal Love*—it's all bunk! Don't bother with her!
NATASHA
    What's that to you? Better hold your tongue—if you have no heart left in you.
NASTYA
    (Fiercely.) You Godforsaken empty man! Where's your soul?
LUKA
    (Taking NASTYA by the arm.) come along, dear. Don't mind them—calm yourself. I know—I believe you. Yours is the truth, not theirs. If you believe you had a real love, then you did have it—you certainly did... [Act III]

In other more serious contexts Luka however comes off rather as pathetic and powerless, however sincere, the way a non swimmer, helpless to save a drowning man, might shed useless tears. Luka surely recognizes this,

his own fatuity and uselessness, as well as that of the role he has been playing as he listens to the screams of Natasha, being punished, like an innocent out of Dostoevsky, by the force majeure of her older sister and the landlord just for wanting to escape from her condition of domestic slavery. All Luka can do then is whine regretfully, indulging in the wishful thinking that Peppel would come back soon:

> BUBNOV
> They do beat her an awful lot now.
> SATIN
> Come on, old man—we'll be witnesses.
> LUKA
> (following SATIN.) I'm no good as a witness—no![4] If only Vassily [Peppel] would come quick—

Luka's words have become helpless before the enormity of the despair around him. The verbal dimension here is de-emphasized, for words at this level of human misery can only either simulate a false hope or represent a position that is already obvious, by the social, cultural and physical place (including body) from which the speaker is talking. We have seen the words fall away before from the ending of Hauptmann's *Weavers*, when the 'people' rush from the entrance hall, symbolically, out into the public reality and contingency of the street, into a life that must change or end.

So here it is the Actor, hanging himself, in the last wordless action of the play, who turns out to be more eloquent in his taciturnity than the articulate Satin (not to mention the garrulous do-gooder Luka), who curses the suicide, for ruining a good drinking song! The rest is silence. Long before *No Exit*, the world of Maxim Gorky's *The Lower Depths* is one from which there is no escape from "the Hell that is other people". Some of the lodgers, like the thief Peppel, seem to have private rooms—whether because crime pays a bit, or because he has been the landlady's lover and they fuck there—but most seem to 'live' in a central common space, where people 'work', play cards, drink lots, argue, argue, argue, perhaps running out of the door into the hall or outside into the street for a break, or ducking under a table or onto a stove to be out of sight—but still not out of hearing range! A total vulnerability reigns in this common space, since the landlord, not to mention the landlady (!), can come in at any time, challenging the right of the lodgers to be there, either because of insolvency or some behavior that's suddenly unacceptable, or of course 'raising the rent'. Even although the rooms, presumably of single occupancy, with doors facing out, may afford some shred of privacy, they allow no secrecy. Anyone coming or going does so in the full view and hearing of all. So the whole inn would know when the landlady is visiting Peppel and can advise the curious husband more or less discreetly or cruelly as to the whereabouts of his straying wife. Ironically, the only real worker in the play, Klestch, some kind of freelance locksmith, who is seen and heard grinding rusty keys throughout Act I, obviously lives, works, and sleeps, along with his dying wife, Anna, in the common space. Anna, in fact, mostly lies in a bed—with a few feeble assisted sorties into the hall or kitchen, for a current of fresh air or to get away from the others—moaning and groaning, agonizing in full view of all during the first two acts, finally, mercifully slipping quietly, almost unnoticed into death. When, early on, she asks for some quiet so she can die in peace, she is told, bluntly "noise never stopped anybody from dying" [Act I].    Basically this setting of structural commonality rips the mask off bourgeois privacy, as well as the sense of identity and entitlement that went with it. Privacy is just another commodity in a world of scarcity, to be bought by those whose class position enables them to deprive others of it.

Overall, what links Gorky's play most tightly to naturalism is the sense of the characters' determination by their environment, their pasts and the past of their species and their class—as evidenced by the very precise indications we just about always get here as to what they did or do or don't do for a living—who their parents were or what they imagine them to have been. Characters in Gorky's play, as in naturalistic theatre generally, as we've noticed, for instance, in Strindberg's blatantly proto-psychoanalytical *Miss Julie*, are constantly referring to their past as an explanation/apology for what they are in the present and in anticipation of a future, or more likely, lack of one.

The one exception to this strict rule of the iron reign of circumstance is the nomadic 'mystic' Luka,, a kind of secular messiah, who, if *The Lower Depths* may be regarded as a godless version of *The Power of Darkness*, would fill some of the place, at least, of Tolstoy's missing redeemer. Of the plays we've been discussing probably the closest to it in fact, and even history and mood, even if not in political consciousness, is Tolstoy's *Power of Darkness*, which Gorky must have known well and admired, as he doubtless wanted to be admired by its author.[5]    These *Lower Depths*, however, would be, for Tolstoy, a world of darkness, without the premise or the promise of Tolstoy's Christian redeemer, certainly without the resolution and hope of any kind of concluding confession. Here death just happens and if Jesus even gets mentioned, for instance by Luka, of course, on his finding Anna dead, on the occasion it's equally clear that's only as a formality or a consolation. All of Luka's statements, *unlike* those of the religious character in Tolstoy's play, the holy and holier-than-thou Akim, father of the promiscuous young sinner, Nikita—are modified by an uncertainty factor, since he is not only a publicly identified liar, but also a self-confessed one. Not that certain shreds of the idea of there being a truth don't remain, as in the aporia or paradox as to whether a liar can be believed when he says he's lying!

This strange and stranger Luka is latest come of the lodgers and earliest departed (not counting Anna, feet first).    Unknown and unknowable are where he's from, what, if anything he's done for a living, what his parentage, descendence, prospects, even beliefs are. The identity, meaning, significance and purpose of Luka are all open to conjecture and were obviously very much meant to be. Doubtless his author himself didn't understand him fully, the way a parent may not understand his own child. As well as certainly more than a hint of the later, world-redeeming Tolstoy, the contemporary Symbolist movement and theatre come to mind: Maeterlinck, Lugné-Poe, the later André Antoine and Strindberg; or, more directly relating to Gorky's context, the important offshoot of Russian Symbolism, in which the mystical figure of the wanderer would have a certain resonance—for instance in Valerii Briusov's later play *The Wayfarer* (1910).[6] We need to remember that this is not only the age of Marxism, materialism, naturalism and rising revolution, but also of much mystical speculation, divagation and experimentation: that of Yeats and Blavatsky, and closer to home, the mystics, Rozanov and Solovyov in Russia. Desperate times produce desperate, sometimes extravagant recourses. Since *The Lower Depths*, with its vast cast and wide range of characters is obviously meant to be representative of the society of the time, its essentially lumpenproletariat cast welcoming the flotsam and jetsam from all classes of society, I think it's also legitimate to see in the figure, behavior and discourse of Luka elements of this apocalyptic religiosity and mysticism. He may as well represent the well-meaning but powerless and helpless god of the Gnostics, as the "hidden god" of the Jansenists, or even Cabalists, the *ain soph* whose "withdrawal" behind the line of further human contact would be tantamount to an abandonment of his creation. Indeed Luka, who has appeared, suddenly and unannounced, equipped with all the wisdom and insight of the omniscient deity (or traditional author!), leaves just as suddenly as he arrived, destination unknown and no forwarding address. We know about him only what we could gather as well from a glance at a stranger we'd never see again: sex, age—he's around 60, and not much more. His lack of identity and civil status are underscored frequently in the play by the demand(s) made on him *passim*, to see his passport, an item he's evidently not supplied with or eager to show, although once or twice he promises, without delivering, to show it soon.

However, that he's a man from nowhere, and going there, doesn't mean he's a man without a message and some kind of mission; and the message and the mission are hope. A society may be able to do without any real hope, but no society can do without the thought, image or illusion of hope; and Luka is the superman of hope. As long as you can dream a little, or need to, he will tell you the story you need or want to hear. His allegiance, he bluntly announces many times, and the more intelligent characters are very well aware of this too, is not to the truth, but to the human being, encouraging our doomed species being of course, unfortunately, always more or less a matter of lying.

Aside from being very much of a political and philosophical statement about its time, one that was understood as subversive of the social order, certainly correctly, given that so many of the participants in the production, as well as Gorky himself, were to serve time subsequently in the Tsar's prisons, *The Lower Depths* is surely a watershed in the evolution of a literary genre, being a true Mississippi of a play, a mighty symphonic confluence of the streams of naturalistic drama we have been following so far. Here an adulterous wife plans, as in *Thérèse Raquin*, to have her lover kill her husband, although, Gorky, distinctly more Nietzschean than Zola, would allow for no role for any kind of 'guilty conscience' in this affair... Also, as in Ibsen's *Ghosts*, there is here a haunting sense of the stifling influence of social conventions, traditions and conformity on the lives of the characters, whose efforts either to adjust to their circumstances or rebel against them bring on crises they are ill equipped to deal with. Sexual or romantic outlets, or fantasies thereof, as attempted solutions to or escapes from the injuries of class are here foregrounded, with results as disappointing, if not as catastrophic as in Strindberg's *Miss Julie*. Explicit, even ideological class consciousness imbues this play as utterly as it did Hauptmann's *Weavers*; but here the focus is on the 'rifraff', or lumpenproletariat—or those without even their 'chains to lose'! Accordingly, consciousness of class, especially where it is essentialist—that is where belief, relaying religion, is in one's unquestionably belonging to one or another category, is always one degree or another of "false consciousness", given the fluidity of things and a controlling vision of a classless society—to come someday! So little Méténier-type exemplary comedies of "false consciousness"—that of individuals whose pretentious ideas about themselves no longer (or never did) correspond to their situation, are scattered throughout the play too, as, for instance, when the Baron, who has been reminiscing about the privileges of his noble ancestors, who had "hundreds of serfs—horses—cooks" is urged by the Voltairian Satin to "forget about your grandfather's carriages. In the carriages of the past you can't go anywhere." [Act IV]! The desolate setting of the play, a dilapidated boarding-house-inn, says it all already, before a word has been spoken. Here, what are called "former people", those who have fallen from a social position, or who never occupied much of one, live jumbled up in a promiscuous hodge-podge or amorphous mass.

Here we are at the bottom of society, but, like the floor of an ocean there are many elements scattered around that used to float serenely on the surface, each with its own point of view as to what it is doing down there. In this sense *The Lower Depths* is very much a theatre of ideas and quite dialogical, affording a overview of competing theories and attitudes about a disintegrating world and prospects of a new one that are far from foregone conclusions. This early in the century, in this signal play, although the proletarian view is a forceful presence through Klestch the freelance keygrinder and the Tartar and Goiter, manual laborers, it seems to me far from dominant or controlling. Other perspectives seem quite as valid and promising. If the criminality of the thief and lover Peppel is doubtless a dead end, so is the realm of private property generally, as represented by the totally unsympathetic inn-owning couple; the acutely intellectual humanist anarchism of Satin is a surer guide to the meaning of the play. He is more of an interpreter to the audience, than Luka, belonging more to 'this world', and so being more comprehensible; it is he, who in fact, pronounces the fundamentally favorable judgment on Luka, late in the play, translating the latter's idealism into a practical "philosophy of man":

> ...The old man had a head on his shoulders. He had the same effect on me as acid on an old, dirty coin....The old man lives from within—he looks at everything through his own eyes. I asked him once: "Grandpa, what do people live for? (*trying to imitate* LUKA'S *voice and manner.*) : They live for something better to come..." ... *A* man can believe or not believe—it's his own affair. A man is free—he pays for everything himself—for belief and disbelief, for love, for intelligence, and that makes him free. Man—that's the truth. What is man? It's not you, nor I, nor they—No, it's you, I, they, the old man, Napoleon, Mohammed—all in one, (*Outlines the figure of man in the air.*) You understand? It's tremendous! In this are all the beginnings and all the ends. Everything in man, everything for man. Only man exists, the rest is the work of his hands and brain. Man! It's magnificent. It has a proud ring!. Man! We have to respect man, not pity him, not demean him—Respect him, that's what we have to do.... [Act IV][7]

But Satin is at his most provocative when sounding like a combination of Bakunin, Kropotkin and Dostoevsky (of iconoclastic narrator of *Notes from Underground*!) he demolishes the sacrosanct concept of work, baiting the pathetic unemployed Klestch, just like a mischievous latter day Voltaire suggesting to some true-believer of a Jesuit that Jesus might have been merely human:

SATIN
  Hey, widower! Why so down in the dumps? What's on your mind?
KLESTCH
  I'm trying to think what to do. I've no tools. The funeral swallowed up everything.
SATIN
  I'll give you a word of advice—don't do anything. Just let yourself be a burden on the world at large!
KLESTCH
  You with your talk. I have some shame before other people.
SATIN
  Forget it. People aren't ashamed at your living worse than a dog. Think this over—you stop working—I stop—hundreds and thousands of others—everybody—understand?—everybody stops working. Nobody wants to do any work—what'll happen then? [Act III]

However much of an anarchist one is, there is always someone even more so. Here this role is filled by the Baron, déclassé aristocrat, whose vice was and continues to be gambling, though he seems to have branched out into pimping (Nastya). The very reality of the world dissolves in the Baron's melancholy, Schopenhaurian non-nostalgia:

> You know, ever since I can remember myself I've always felt a sort of fog in my head. I could never understand anything. I have an awkward feeling as if all my life I've done nothing but change clothes—But to what end? I can't figure it out. I was given an education, wore the uniform of a college for the nobility—but what did I study? I don't remember. I got married—to a woman who was no good, wore tails, then a dressing gown—why? I don't know. I went through my fortune—came to wear an old gray jacket and faded pants—But how did I go broke? I didn't notice. I got a job on a government board—wore a uniform, a cap with a badge—then embezzled government money, had prison clothes put on me, and later changed into this. And all that as if in a dream. It's funny. [Act IV]

This anarchism of Satin, or nihilism of the Baron, not to mention the mystical (if essentially secular, whatever the religious vocabulary it is cloaked in) idealism of Luka might seem arguably less than proletarian in inspiration and direction. Dramatically and especially naturalistically, Gorky is certainly representing a range of views. Communism, although very much on the horizon, has not been much more than an interesting experiment when Gorky was creating this play—in 1902, what with the bloody defeats of the class war of 1848 and the Paris Commune of 1870. Here, the proletarian worker's voice, although very much of a presence, is by no means the controlling and authoritative one. Shrewder, more intellectual, cynical and even mystical voices seem to speak as compellingly. Yet, in another way it is conceivable to think of Gorky as more faithful to the spirit of Marx in his very infidelity. I'm thinking of the leitmotif, in the early Marx, of the proletariat being the (only) class that is called upon to abolish the class system as such, as well as the system of private property on which it is based, since its protest is not against any *particular* injustice but against injustice as such. Nothing Marx ever said I think had a greater impact than this, still well remembered around the time of the French May '68, that revolution-for-nothing, as paraphrased (from Marx's "Introduction to Contribution to Critique of Hegel's *Philosophy of Law*") so memorably by the dynamic, nervy and catalytic Guy Debord:

> No quantitative relief of its poverty, no illusory hierarchical incorporation, can supply a lasting cure for its dissatisfaction; for the proletariat cannot truly recognize itself in any particular wrong it has suffered; nor, therefore, *in the righting of any particular wrong*—nor even in the righting of many such wrongs; but only in the righting of the *unqualified wrong* that has been perpetrated upon it—the universal wrong of its exclusion from life. [p. 85; pp. 76-77, 1969 French ed.][8]

This melting pot of *The Lower Depths*, as well as a brutally realistic depiction of the cruelties and injuries of the present-day world, would also be utopian and prophetic, a kind of vision of a classless society. Disrespectful in the extreme, as prime example of this utopian quality, is the attitude of Gorky's characters toward money, the closest thing to a sacrament there is in capitalist culture, defied with such vituperation, for instance by Marx in the *Economic and Philosophical Manuscripts of 1844*:

> Money, then, appears as this *distorting* power both against the individual and against the bonds of society, etc., which claim to be *entities* in themselves. It transforms fidelity into infidelity, love into hate, hate into love, virtue into vice, vice into virtue, servant into master, master into servant, idiocy into intelligence, and intelligence into idiocy. Since money, as the existing and active concept of value, confounds and confuses all things, it is the general *confounding* and *confusing* of all things—the world upside down—the confounding and confusing of all natural and human qualities.[9]

Essential to any kind of Marxist or Communist vision of a better world must be the more or less immediate abrogation of money and the dehumanization and alienation it stands for. *Utopian*[10] then, and looking forward to a classless society is the fact that, with the exception of the repudiated inn-owners, a more or less total insouciance toward cash is indeed typical of everyone else in the play: one senses that even the thief steals not for gain, but for want of something else to do with himself; money for the Baron is just something to gamble with; for Satin and the Actor merely a few kopecks to be begged or wheedled for drink[11]; while Luka, like Socrates, was suspect by reason of the very gratuitousness of his generous advice!

Without leaving the grim world of the gutter, where the honesty of the naturalistic theatre, of which it is such a noble extension, requires it remain—to represent an unredeemed, exploited humanity—Gorky's play represents a step beyond, expressed by the dramatic conception of characters who have attained a level of consciousness capable of generating the capacity to refuse to be bought and sold by a society that buys and sells everything and everyone else. The theatre of Gorky here remains, nevertheless, solidly naturalistic, not crossing over into the vaguer terrain of its influential contemporary, Symbolism, because the denizens of these *Lower Depths*, however unworldly, are not 'otherworldly'. They are fugitives, nomads, wanderers on the face of the earth, lost in our cities and forever ready to run. Yet although they pay in kind (health, security, anxiety) for their freedoms, they do not let their vulnerability stop them from doing what they can for each other, acting, drinking, consoling, confronting in solidarity a common threat or class enemy (landlords, police etc.) whenever there is an opportunity. Gorky's play remains uncompromisingly, even strictly naturalistic, since its characters, at their best, and of course, with varying degrees of success or failure, start the "revolution" while remaining within their world and situation, with modifications in prevailing attitudes, as in their indifference toward money; and in the nearly total lack of prevalence among them of the bourgeois dream of enrichment and privilege.  If they escape it's to the idea and the incipient practice of a better or future world *within this one*, yielding up even to the temptation of the idea of heaven, if at all, only at the moment of death, as in Luka's thoroughly 'situational' consolation of the publicly dying Anna.

The world of *The Lower Depths* may be assumed to be lower and more abject even than that of its public generally (no one at the inn talks about going to the theatre!), a representation of a reality belonging to the past and present of humanity; but there is also a sense in which it is something 'higher', having transcended bourgeois consciousness, according to which everything would be convertible into and exchangeable for cash.  For here not everything, not everyone is for sale; and there is more than an intimation that something better can and does start right here and now, with the refusal of characters, preeminently Luka's, to accept remuneration for their giving. Luka, who trades his love only for love, along with the insightful Satin, a 'chorus' who ultimately expounds Luka's message and meaning, then are living promises and embodiments of the other side of the 'coin of the money society' Marx provides a fabulous 'promised land' glimpse of in the *Manuscripts of 1844*:

Assume *man* to be *man* and his relationship to the world to be a human one: then you can exchange love only for love, trust for trust, etc.  If you want to enjoy art, you must be an artistically cultivated person; if you want to exercise influence over other people, you must be a person with a stimulating and encouraging effect on other people.  Every one of your relations to man and to nature must be a *specific expression*, corresponding to the object of your will, of your *real individual* life.  If you love without evoking love in return—that is, if your loving as loving does not produce reciprocal love; if through a *living expression* of yourself as a loving person you do not make yourself a *beloved one*, then your love is impotent—a misfortune. [Marx and Engels, Vol. 3, p. 326][12]

# VII. A Living Like Any Other: *Mrs. Warren's Profession*

"If, as Chesterton said, Shaw is the first idealist who is not also a sentimentalist, might one add that he is the first unsentimental naturalist?"

—Eric Bentley[1]

A young Englishwoman (Vivie Warren), ostensibly upper class, finds out what her mother (Mrs. Warren) really does for a living (runs a brothel in Brussels, in partnership with a wealthy male admirer), how she has been supported and educated, and who her true father might be (the Reverend Samuel Gardner, next door, former lover/client of her mother), in the process discovering that her fiancé, Frank (the Reverend's son), might well be her half-brother...

The play, *Mrs. Warren's Profession*, written in 1893, Shaw says in a stormy preface, was meant for the naturalized Dutchman's, Jacob T Grein's Independent Theatre[2], of London, modeled after theatres in Paris and Berlin that were staging naturalist plays. Grein was courageous enough, for example, to have produced Ibsen's *Ghosts* there in 1891, which resulted in the tidal wave of critical outrage Shaw delineates so amusingly in *The Quintessence of Ibsenism*.[3] Grein, apparently, was far from happy with *Mrs. Warren's Profession*, especially after it failed to receive the necessary approval of the Lord Chamberlain for performance. Grein, who liked Ibsen and other continental firebrands, and who actually had produced a play of Shaw's previously (his first, *Widower's House*), reproached the author with "shattering his ideals."[4] The problem for Grein, was that Shaw's handling of Mrs. Warren did not really connect her with any blame, or immorality, since the play's 'message', in fact, is that individuals being pretty much obliged to be what they are, moral judgments are irrelevant, if not impertinent and unfair. Mrs. Warren is unhappy, of course, at the end of the play, simply because her daughter has decided to have nothing further to do with her— this decision, however, is unconnected really with blame or even shame: the "apple does not fall far from the tree", an apt naturalist maxim, means here that Vivie will make this decision to break with her mother for the same reasons that her mother decided to go into the 'profession' of prostitution—because it was the most practical of choices, given the kind of society we live in. Women who make their own decisions, or try to, in matters of the heart and otherwise, in literature, from Cleopatra and Phaedra, through Juliet, to Madame Bovary, Anna Kerenina, Hedda Gabler and Miss Julie have always served as negative examples, whatever passions and admirations they aroused, ending up unhappily, almost always by suicide, dying of poison, under a train, or taking a knife or a gun to themselves, just to mention the particular sad, if, *then and there* culturally required ends of these; not so, Mrs. Warren who is unquestionably going to live on, and is going to continue along the line she has been "obliged to choose". Prostitution, anyway, far from being exceptional is the way of today's world, in Eric Bentley succinct formula: "Capitalism...is but a polite word for prostitution. Mrs. Warren's profession is only the most dramatic example..." (p. 6)

So the play, refused permission, could not be performed publicly in London until 1925, although there was a private performance there in 1902 (arousing the outrage Shaw delineates in his later preface); and it was staged by Arnold Daly in 1905, in New York, about which Shaw says: "The press of that city instantly raised a cry that such persons as Mrs. Warren are 'ordure' and should not be mentioned in the presence of decent people," ("Preface", p. 27) with the result that Daly and the company were arrested (Daly was eventually acquitted, but meanwhile further performances, because of delays and expenses, had to be cancelled).

Allowances must be made for how disturbing it may have been to see upper class people being as frankly honest (if not cynical), if not more so, about their options and choices in terms of what they do for money as lower class people. The cynical carpenter, Engstrand, for example, from *Ghosts*, who after marrying another man's mistress, wants to set his 'daughter' up in the brothel business, either did not know any better or could not afford to; but what are we to think of the equally cynical and opportunistic *Sir* George Crofts of Shaw's play, Mrs. Warren's business partner, former (maybe current) lover, and would-be seducer-fiancé of the daughter, and who is quite open about his past actions and future intentions? What is thereby undercut by such 'honesty' is the whole rationale and legitimacy of the entitlement of one class to privileges and perquisites denied to another, based on a supposed moral ascendancy. That said, *Mrs. Warren's Profession* must have shocked and challenged for reasons other than what happens or doesn't happen ('vice' punished, 'virtue' rewarded) in the play, for surely it is the most "polite" and "civilized" of the plays in our naturalist procession so far: here there is no husband being murdered by a pair of adulterous lovers, no young man with everything to live for begging his mother to help him die as the sins of the father are visited on the son in the form of the onset of inherited syphilis, no unwanted baby smothered, young woman seduced and 'suicided', workers sacking the factory, or lumpenproletariat jumbled up promiscuously at a dead-end inn.  Strangely, it might be closest in mood to the little anarchist-communist skits of Oscar Méténier, created and performed in Paris  just about the time that Shaw's play was being interdicted by the Lord Chamberlain.  In Méténier's work the subject is, as it always is in Shaw, consciousness, more specifically—false consciousness:   The future sire in *Little Bugger* has been thinking like a capitalist in wanting to name his child after himself, not as the propertyless proletarian he is who "has nothing to lose but his chains", as he realizes, coming to his senses, at the end of the mini epiphany that constitutes the playlet.  So Shaw operates by moving his characters, insofar as they can be moved, in their minds, decisions and articulations, a clear step closer to their reality—which is their rootedness in and determination by the economy—in other words, by *money*.

We have seen how money was conspicuous by its absence or lack of importance attached to it in what we have conceived of as a kind of virtual Communist utopia of Gorky's *Lower Depths*, which was being adored in Moscow at about the same time (1902) that *Mrs. Warren's Profession*, after a private performance, was being excoriated in London.  However, in the dream-logic of the literary, *a fortiori*, theatrical realm, revolutionary denial, or hyperbolic, ironic and cynical affirmation and acceptance amount to the same thing, representing merely two sides of the same "coin"—so here, in Shaw's play, money is conspicuous by its overwhelming presence and its totally controlling impact.  The world of *Mrs. Warren* is the reverse image of the (under)world of *The Lower Depths*, but one that has no need of a redeemer, such as Luka plays at being in Gorky's play, because it already has been redeemed, albeit in the sense of an item redeemed in a pawnshop.  The world has been redeemed and exchanged for money, a fact as plain as the nose on your face, or the Emperor's new clothes; *Mrs. Warren* representing the worst fears and prophecies of the (early) Marx about "the world turned upside down" of money, the all destroyer, all-leveler, come true.

*Mrs. Warren*, of course, builds upon, without just repeating, both the Darwinian and Marxist qualities of the previous naturalistic drama, of which it is an extension; but its difference lies in the fact that where the other naturalist plays act things out, this play thinks things out.  Here, as in Shaw's theatre generally, discussion is maximal, action is minimal; the consciousness it aims at raising is in fact a conscious awareness, preliminary to a kind of conscience.

Naturalism, in theatre as well as fiction, had always been attracted to the animal in man and the proletarian in the economy; it had been fond of lust, alcoholism, poverty and revolution.  In terms of the awesome psychological paradigm Sigmund Freud was developing contemporaneously with it, its realm would be that of the unconscious, that is the id, with all that connotes in terms of the untrammeling of the libido and the nakedness and violence of

the will to survival and to power.  This is why its favorite milieu had always
been the lower classes of society—the poor, the sick, the 'insulted and the
injured', living closer to their instincts and hungers (because they are
hungry).  Naturalism's ideal type is the "human beast" of Zola, or to turn to
his American disciples, Crane and Norris: the helpless young prostitute,
*Maggie, Girl of the Streets*, the panicked soldier of *The Red Badge of
Courage*, or in *McTeague*, the pathetic dumb giant of a self-educated dentist
who rips out teeth with his bare hands.  Additionally, the 'déclassé', whether
they have been ruined emotionally like Miss Julie in Strindberg's play, or
economically like the Baron in Gorky's, or "destroyed by love", like
Hurstwood, in Dreiser's *Sister Carrie*, are favored, for they have tumbled
into the lower orders, into the slime where they must fight like animals for
their lives and/or die like dogs.

However, to stay with Freud's paradigm, Shaw's provocation in this play
was to lift naturalism from the level of the unconscious to that of the
conscious, from the id to the ego (and superego)—where we calculate,
reason, exploit and manipulate in full awareness of what we are doing and
why; which is why it is threatening and dangerous on a whole new level.
Here we have, for instance, a mother and daughter separating for life, not
after a display of naked animal emotion, but coldly and rationally.  In the
final scene of the play Vivie adjourns her mother because it is in her own
"best interest", and Mrs. Warren is obliged to admit, by her very own
standards, that she was right in doing so:

VIVIE
...I am right, am I not?...I should be a fool not to
MRS. WARREN
(*sulkily*): Oh, well, yes, if you come to that, I suppose you are

Shaw's clear escalation in the realm of naturalism in this play, an
obvious offshoot of that 'tradition'—but this I think applies to his theatre
generally (for instance, the critique and downplaying of 'lust' and 'romance',
thematic in his work)—was to move the arena of internal (psychological) and
external (social) struggle, conflict and stress from the domain of the
unconscious to that of consciousness, where it becomes clear that those same
forces, economic, environmental, genetic and accidental  that shaped our
unconscious drives and energies also create our conscious thoughts, 'choices
and decisions'.  The consciousness, therefore, that Shaw raises is that all
social classes, all portions of the psyche (Freudian, if you will) are equally
oppressed by a system, from which there is no shelter or asylum and that
allows no exceptions to its iron, inhuman rule.

Shaw's patient, industrious Fabianism, or confidence in the prospects of
gradual change, as opposed to sudden revolutionary violence comes into
clear dramatic focus here.  As opposed, then, to the outraged naturalism of

such theatre as *The Weavers* and *The Lower Depths*, whereby more or less literally a lower and/or under-class "storms the Bastille" of society in order to effect immediate, cataclysmic change, Shaw's 'civilized' naturalism is more about raising the temperature of the political waters to the boiling point, so that change happens almost of itself, therefore having more of a chance of being established on a more stable basis, because the need for such has been accepted on more universal grounds than the interests of any particular strata.

Class posture, pretension and pride evaporate then in the bright sun of Shaw's searing honesty and the heat of never-slackening mockery, resulting—virtually and imaginatively—in a melting and a merging of all classes into one. In the realm of reality, from which, diverting and entertaining as it is, Shaw's theatre provides no escape, there would be no sense in attacking each other—since we're all in the same boat, and a hole in the bottom would only sink us all. The thing is to keep it afloat and going, then limping, if need be, back into port for repairs...then out to sea again.

# VIII. A Naturalist Symbolism: *Riders to the Sea*

*Riders to the Sea* (1903-4), J. M. Synge's strange, brief (one-act) lamentation of a play is set in a desolate (treeless) windswept, forgotten (until the Irish revival rediscovered it) corner of the cosmos, one of the Aran Islands, off the northwest coast of Ireland. This work shows us indeed the total victory of the cosmos over man's puny inventions and ambitions, with some consolation maybe to be derived in the poetry of the acceptance of this; the stage, which had moved out into proletarian revolution (Hauptmann), lower class and lumpen-proletariat city-scape (Méténier-Antoine, Gorky), peasant misery (Tolstoy) and out into the economy (Shaw) now extends to nature, as represented by its least controllable aspect, the sea. One has the feeling, with *Riders to the Sea*, that the stage here is only the vestibule of an elemental world that cannot be shown due to its very scope and vastness. The stage takes on the temporary aspect of a rock-in-the-middle-of-the-sea, from which one can observe the working of the forces of nature. Before such forces no free will is possible and no individual can stand; the only reasonable attitude would be that of resignation:

> MAURYA
> (*raising her head and speaking as if she did not see the people around her*):
> They're all gone now, and there isn't anything more the sea can do to me....I'll have no call now to be up crying and praying when the wind breaks from the south, and you can hear the surf is in the east, and the surf is in the west....and I won't care what way the sea is when the other women will be keening.[1]

Language is no longer only human communication, assuming it ever was just that, but has become lamentation, addressed as it must be to the heavens, gods, or whatever personal or impersonal entities that, whether or not they exist, would have to be invented for that purpose, for humanity needs something or someone to cry out to, if only a hallucinated being. The verbal content of such a theatre only serves to point the way to an essentially wordless experience: our shared helplessness before conditions that are out of our power to control. Any vestigial gap remaining between stage and audience left by the remorseless naturalism of a theatre that has been assaulting this division, through theatralizing domestic life, night life, factory work, peasants, prostitutes, "lower depth" inns of social devolution into a primordial classless ooze—just about since the Paris Commune and French Civil War (between the classes) of 1870—dissolves in the existential statement about the human condition that must be generalized from the particular situation of these keening Aran woman, bereft by the sea of all the men in their lives: we are all equally at the disposal of external forces, whether natural or social, against which, though we may rage, we can never prevail.

The logical concomitant of this mutual blending, which we have been describing, of audience and stage, or of stage and a previously separate reality, has been a gradual de-emphasizing of the individuality of the characters, who become mere representatives of forces that surpass and eventually suppress them. Synge tells us above that Maurya is *"speaking as if she did not see the people around her"*. She is essentially alone on a stage where individuals have ceased to exist, as the stage has become a cosmos which has swallowed them up.[2]

The action of the play is minimal; one can hardly imagine one—aside from those of the symbolist Maeterlinck who exerted doubtless an influence on Synge, competitive certainly with that of the naturalists—before Beckett (who is in a direct line of descent, culturally and artistically from Synge anyway) where less happens: essentially an older woman (Maurya) and her daughters are waiting around to hear confirmation that a son (Michael) who has been missing at sea has been drowned. While his effects are being found and identified, her last remaining son and man in her life, Bartley, leaves to attend a horse fair, on the way to which he will be drowned in turn. Bartley's 'reported' drowning, recalls the fated (through his father, Theseus' sentence) death of Hippolytus, destroyed by Neptune (Poseidon) in Euripides' play by that name and Racine's *Phèdre*. Thus Synge adheres to the classical tragic unity of action of Aristotle, whereby death is reported rather than witnessed by the audience. All the same. this scene is one of the most 'lively' moments in the play. Maurya, in the end, has lost all the men in her life to the sea:

> There was Sheamus and his father, and his own father again, were lost in a dark night, and not a stick or sign was seen of them when the sun went up. There was Patch after was drowned out of a curagh that turned over. I was sitting here with Bartley, and he a baby, lying on my two knees, and I seen two women, and three women and four women coming in, and they crossing themselves, and not saying a word. (p. 10)

Basically the men all drown and the women are left keening. Some of the minimal action of the play is involved with the concern of Maurya's two daughters, Cathleen and Nora, in their efforts to hide a bundle of what might be (what almost certainly is) the missing-at-sea Michael's effects from being noticed by his mother, Maurya, until they are absolutely sure, or they deem she's more ready to hear about it. Another slight crease of action involves their (mother and daughters concerting) efforts to persuade Bartley, who will be drowned during the course of the play, not to leave, but of course, in vain. Basically any action in the play is merely the formality of a show of attempting to keep fate at bay, in a world in which everything important, basically anything to do with life or death, has already been decided. So, dramatically, action, involving decision, here yields to ritual, where tradition takes over and spectacle consoles, excites and finally soothes.

Accordingly, the central moment here belongs to no one individual but the scenery and pictorial 'music' of the chorus of women who come in with the report of Bartley's end and the men who later bring his very body as:

> ...the old women begin to come in, crossing themselves on the threshold, and kneeling down in front of the stage with red petticoats over their heads....The women are keening softly and swaying themselves with a slow movement. (p. 10)

If theatre was born, among the ancient Greeks, as a protest of man against the 'injustice' of his circumstances, with the hope and by setting the example he can do something about them—as in 6th century Athens the Hypocrite emerges from the chorus of Dionysian goat-singers, prelude to the three dimensional characters that debate issues and problems in the 5th century drama of Aeschylus, Sophocles and Euripides, here it seems that theatre is sinking back into the ritual and anonymity whence it arose. Significantly it is this ritual aspect that seems to move the heart and soul of Maurya from an attitude of bitter defiance and rebellion to one of calmer resignation and acceptance: "No man at all can be living for ever and we must be satisfied", are Maurya's and the play's last words.

The dramatic conflict here was not so much between characters with different points of view, or (class) interests as between different approaches to the theatre of life: on the one hand the naturalist environment that pits men against each other and ultimately against the cosmos; on the other hand, a profoundly symbolic dimension in which one not only accepts a sad fate, but outbidding catastrophe, celebrates, commemorates and even revels in it.

Certainly neither the action of the play, nor its framework of tragic inevitability and pathos identifies it as modern, but especially the extremely humble social status of the characters surely does so, together with the "language" they speak, Synge's original version of their Gaelic-English dialect. Such "low" characters, particularly in major roles, would have been inconceivable before the advent of naturalism, except of course as objects of

scorn or mirth, an example of the scorn being Shakespeare's handling of the
John Cade Rebellion in *Henry VI, Part Two*; of the mirth being the slapstick
treatment of the worker-players in *Midsummer Night's Dream*; things start to
change by the end of the 'revolutionary' 18th century, it's true, with the
advent of the ambitious barber in Beaumarchais' play, then Mozart's opera,
*The Marriage of Figaro*, but there it was still a case of the traditional
attempts to rise in social class, not dealing with any 'lower' class in its own
terms.   An exception to this rule was the strangely "materialist drama",[3]
*Woyzeck* (1836), by George Büchner, where the patently underclass
protagonist is portrayed as being deprived of his mate, his pride and,
outrageously, his sanity by the implacable and cruel injustices of the social
class system, as represented by one of its most blatant embodiments, the
military.   Yet Büchner, accepting the challenges and writing in the wake of
what was most radical about the French Revolution (say the expunged
anarchist element of Gracchus Babeuf), was in turn, very vitally in the
current that led to the concept of proletarian revolution, of Marx and Engels,
of the *Communist Manifesto*, of 1848, which in turn, after political and
military setbacks and detours, provided much of the framework for the
creation and development of literary, and especially theatrical Naturalism.

   An evident precursor of *Riders to the Sea* as a play of nearly unrelieved
lamentation by women for their 'lost men' is clearly Euripides' *Trojan
Women*, but there the mourners are of noble rank; not so here, where, if
anything, it's the elemental, universal reality of what is being expressed,
concerning the loss of loved ones, that is 'noble' and those through whom we
can most readily grasp this *fatum* its most effective embodiments.
Anticipating Naturalism in this sense, a certain 'naïve and sentimental'
Romanticism saw people of humble station, and/or else children, as being
closer to the feelings connected with such a reality than people of higher
social rank, protected by their education and the rationalizations that come
with it, from direct contact with their feelings, or even recognizing them
often as such.   In other words, profound emotions—the deepest of which
must be attached to the loss of loved ones, as in *Riders*, would be more
clearly and sincerely expressed by uneducated, even illiterate people, those
who haven't been equipped with consoling theories and explanatory ideas to
come between themselves and their sorrow.   Such is the logic behind much
of Wordsworth's poetry, whose subjects are shepherds, aged impoverished
survivors, mourners, farmer folk or country laborers.   The major statement of
this novel point of view was Wordsworth's (later) preface to the watershed
publication of *Lyrical Ballads*, of 1798, to which Samuel Taylor Coleridge
also contributed his poems.   Here is a mood that will eventually be very
much that of Synge's *Riders*, especially on the themes of death and loss.
These are never more intensely felt than through the mother's loss of a son
and/or children's confusion about the sheer fact of mortality, as emphasized
by Wordsworth, who described his purpose to be accomplished:

...by tracing the maternal passion through many of its more subtle windings, as in the poems of the *Idiot Boy* and the *Mad Mother*; by accompanying the last struggles of a human being, at the approach of death, cleaving in solitude to life and society, as in the poem of the *Forsaken Indian*; by shewing, as in the stanzas entitled *We Are Seven*, the perplexity and obscurity which in childhood attend our notion of death, or rather our utter inability to admit that notion... (Wordsworth, p. 1439)

Coincidentally, Coleridge's contributions to this book were poems specifically concerned with the *supernatural*, like *The Rime of the Ancient Mariner*, while the concern of Wordsworth, whose poems tended to be about simple rustic life and characters, was to focus on the *natural*, certainly a precursor to Naturalism; although there would be limits to this analogy, since Wordsworth, as a Romantic, would of course tend to spiritualize matter,[4] no matter how humble (which makes for even more room for spirit). Naturalism, strictly speaking, on the contrary, would tend to materialize any 'matter' reminiscent of spirit.

In Synge's theatre, Naturalism is represented by the reality of the kind of "ordinary" (if exotic and unfamiliar, by reason of their very plainness) characters that tend to make you forget they are "merely acted", the authentic decor and setting, based on his knowledge of the Aran Islands and islanders;[5] the absence of any plot to speak of, except as provided by the great plot of the universe that puts us all into abeyance before the death of others, and of course our own decline and fall, and then the 'common language'[6] in which all this somber fatality is dramatized and articulated. Naturalism in Synge is certainly a dynamic, catalytic, even essential and central element; but it is equally clear that for him Naturalism can only go so far; in a sense, if it is to be consistent with itself it must then self-destruct; for naturalistically, it must be admitted that the naturalist world as such, at times of extreme urgency, in our 'limit moments'—for instance, in and out of love, or else when life and death are at stake, and *a fortiori* in mourning—is uninhabitable. Dostoevskian, in the sense of *Notes from the Underground*, where it is wondered "what if it is in the interest of man *not* to act in his interest", we would have to call this noble 'moment' and situation in Synge's theatre: Where, for example, in *Deirdre of the Sorrows* (1907-9), the lovers choose to return to Ireland to die rather than live on tepidly and safely in Scotland, whence they have eloped[7]; or in *The Well of the Saints* (1903-8), where there is a bluntly Maeterlinckian-Platonic Symbolist dialogue and dialectic between blindness and sight, essence and existence; here, in *The Well of the Saints*, blind beggars, in an additional dimension of Voltairian, Candide-style irony, choose in the end to remain blind, since the world there is to see is such a terribly disappointing one.

What in fact we seem to be confronting in Synge's theatrical practice is a kind of strange marriage between Symbolism and Naturalism, a Symbolic Naturalism, or Naturalist Symbolism, if you will, depending on which you want to emphasize or make the more substantive or substantial. Unquestionably, Synge, who studied in Paris around the same time André Antoine was very active there, was indelibly impressed by both movements. In all of Synge's work the Naturalism is well in evidence, first of all in the prominence of the economic factor—how people do or don't 'make a living', usually a quite lowly one, or at least very ordinary. Even for an apparent exception, *Deirdre of the Sorrows*, medieval-mythic Gaelic in setting and themes, when Deirdre first appears it is said she *"...comes in poorly dressed with a little bag and a bundle of twigs in her arms"*, while in the ensuing dialogue with King Conchubar, who wants to make her his queen, it is at once apparent that she is very humbly a creature of the material world of human need and wants only to stay one:

CONCHUBAR
    What have you brought from the hills?
DEIRDRE
    [*quite self-possessed*] A bag of nuts, and twigs for our fires at the dawn of day.
CONCHUBAR
    [*showing annoyance in spite of himself*] And it's that way you're picking up
the manners will fit you to be Queen of Ulster?
DEIRDRE
    [*made a little defiant by his tone*] I have no wish to be a queen. (p. 154)

In Synge's theatre otherwise we are dealing almost always with people of humble station: tinkers (*The Tinker's Wedding*), beggars (*The Well of the Saints*), inn keepers and farmers who come in for a drink or to get out of the cold (*The Playboy of the Western World*), small country landholders and laborers (*The Shadow of the Glen*), and of course. in *Riders,* the simple Aran islanders, fisherfolk and the women who wait for them (not) to come home.

Also, Naturalism is in evidence in the predominance of emotions, passions, 'animal' lusts and appetites in this theatre. Synge's characters tend to be "id" or instinct driven; given the slightest provocation or incitement (even, comically an imagined one) and men and women are 'all over' each other. It's immediately apparent, for example, that every woman in town, in *Playboy of the Western World* wants to bed the handsome young fugitive parricide, Christopher Mahon; the wife in *The Shadow of the Glen*, who thinks she's already a widow, is entertaining her 'fiancé' while the body of her 'dead' husband is lying on a table in the same cottage room (he has only been pretending to be dead, 'coming back' finally to foil his wife's plans). The comical limit of untrammeled sexual passion has got to be, however, Martin Doul, the formerly and future blind beggar in *The Well of the Saints*, whom people have been lying to, for fun, about how good he looks, who, after rejecting his wife (also formerly blind), whom he can now see is ugly, throws himself at the most nubile and attractive young woman in town, only to be rejected of course, after a moment in which the young woman, *"who has listened half-mesmerized*", hesitates, in a kind of hypnotized trance. This is reminiscent of the comicality of such moments of inappropriate wooings, as for Malvolio in *Twelfth Night* and Tartuffe in Molière's play, except for the fact that Synge's Naturalism here allows for a motion of evident, if involuntary attraction of the seduced toward the seducer, at once complicating the situation and making it more fascinating.

Equally Naturalist is the emphasis on food and conviviality in the plays, and especially drink; and although, of course, drink, abundant to overflowing in the inn-setting of *Playboy of the Western World*, is missing from *Riders*, a kind of bread, which they call 'cake' is being prepared and baked there during the play, according to authentic methods and styles Synge certainly observed first-hand. In other words, in Synge's theatre physical and emotional needs, desires, hungers, sufferings, lusts and yearnings are inescapably primordial and even catalytic; but they don't tell the full story, far from it, and that's where the Symbolism comes in. Symbolic, certainly, for instance, *as well as Naturalist*, is this 'cake' in *Riders*, kneaded and cooked during the play, first meant to feed the returning Michael, who, drowned, won't need it, then meant to accompany Maurya's last man, her son Bartley, on his fateful journey, but failing that (Maurya had meant to give it to him, but preoccupied with her sorrow and resentment had forgotten to, then pursuing him could not catch up), it will be offered to feed the men who are going to make Barley's coffin: "I have a new cake," says Cathleen, Maurya's older daughter, to one of these men, "you can eat it while you'll be working." (p. 10).

Other symbolist elements are: the rope Bartley will take to use as a halter, which his mother will try to dissuade him from taking, since it will be needed to lower the missing and presumably drowned Michael into his "deep grave"; the black knot tying the bundle of Michael's clothes (p. 7), obvious symbol of death; then while we're on black, "the pig with the black feet" that has been eating at the rope, "pigs are associated with death in Irish folklore and black with ill luck or even evil", according to the editor's note (p.188); the grey pony visualized or hallucinated (Bartley has ridden off on a red mare) by Maurya, with her 'drowned' son Michael, alive and well dressed on it:

> Bartley came first on the red mare; and I tried to say 'God speed you,' but something choked the words in my throat. He went by quickly; and 'the blessing of God on you,' says he, and I could say nothing. I looked up then, and I crying, at the grey pony, and there was Michael upon it—with fine clothes on him, and new shoes on his feet. (p.9)

About which the editor, Ann Saddlemyer's note explains:

> The grey horse, its colour ghost-like, is reminiscent of the Pale Horse in Revelations, but in Irish folklore it is also the *puca*, a spirit in the form of a horse

which lures people to their death; in this case the vision is compounded because it
was believed that the dead can return to claim a companion (pp. 189-90)

Finally, for our purposes, but certainly not exhaustively, there are several
references at the end of the play to the pre-Christian "Celtic festival",
Samhain (p. 11), when "it was believed, the spirits of the dead moved freely
among the living." (p. 190)

Here in *Riders*, where Naturalism is at its starkest and most brutally
simple and animal—where the living is at its most basic, a matter of
surviving, and barely, while waiting for the news that those we love the most
have passed on: "...it's only a bit of wet flour we do have to eat, and maybe a
fish that would be stinking." (p. 11), as Maurya announces, the play is
absolutely replete with Symbolism too. As if where the human condition is
at its most unbearably painful, there is the most need to transcend it—or
maybe closest to the virtual revolution, with which it is contemporary,
dramatized as having "always already happened", as we have described it, of
Gorky's *Lower Depths*. There Luka, the rootless, identity-less wanderer
supplies a bit of the yeast of a Symbolist transcendence, or the hope thereof,
as leavening to the bread of existence among the 'insulted and the injured'.

Another way of looking at the problematic of this Symbolist-Naturalism
or Naturalist-Symbolism of *Riders* (and Synge's theatre in general, or even
of the whole project, including the Irish Revival he was so central to, or of
any of the many nationalist or ethnic cultural/political movements of then—
and likely now!) is to view it as blatantly counter-revolutionary, as an
aesthetic-theatrical response to the non-arrival of revolutionary change, or its
failure to occur or its aftermath, perhaps of disillusion with its results (for
instance leading only in a change of masters: bureaucrats and commissars for
tsars and noblemen). Certainly the "common man" is as much if not more in
evidence in the theatre of Synge than anywhere else in the history of theatre,
Naturalism included; and never more so in Synge than in *Riders*, albeit
almost entirely as the women who wait to hear that their men are dead. But
what is missing, as far as Naturalism is concerned, is any proletarian sense of
uniting or organizing to overthrow the order of things and the classes that
rule over such and benefit thereby. Although solidarity is present here and
amply, in the face of the incurable nature of the malady of existence and the
necessity to resign oneself to and accept the inevitable, even to celebrate and
commemorate it, ultimately such revolution as there is is more of a
revolution in the ancient, and etymological sense of the word, a turning back
to a past, even pre-Christian, archaic epoch, before the dissemination of such
ideas as betterment and progress—towards tragedy and the consolations of
fate and destiny. This is when 'time stands still', meaning it cannot be
affected in any meaningful way by the machinations, plans or resentments of
mankind. It seems very much to me that Synge's theatre is split quite along
these lines, and never more utterly and nakedly than in *Riders*: on the one

hand, a profoundly authentic Naturalist framework, as pure and 'elemental' as any in that new tradition we have been surveying since Zola. Because of the organic and visceral ties of the Naturalism, especially of the theatre, with the kind of insurrectionary communism of Marx and Engels, this suggests, if only by powerful implication, the 'return of the repressed' of proletarian/lower class revolution. Yet if a Naturalism as pure as Synge's can't help but convey this 'revolutionary impulse' it can't help but reject or at least postpone it also, as if by reflection on failures and/or impossibilities of political revolutions of the past (1848, 1870) or of those to come, falling back, therefore, artistically and culturally on the premises of a Symbolist alternative; or more exactly developing this alternative concurrently; and this is the genius, beauty and originality of Synge's theatre, as well as one of the sources its deep stress, anguish and passionate tension. It is a place where irreconcilables can coexist, at least momentarily or aesthetically..

So I think it makes sense to say that until the Russian Revolution, which we need to conceive of also as 'happening before it happens' in the minds of artists, poets and dramatists, Naturalism, especially of the theatre, because of its public and structurally social nature, is revolutionary or is not Naturalism. "After the Revolution", whether really or virtually (in anticipatory imagination) when the changeover either has already happened or has failed to happen, or has become one, lets say, in name only—comes the question of what to do with this powerful, combative, political style of Naturalism, when it is no longer cogent, relevant or coherent. Can this weapon of the war between the classes be converted to peacetime uses? But in the service of what class, since the proletariat, following Marx's splendid vision, was the class that was to put an end to class society? Yet if all hope for such a society has been closed off, or postponed indefinitely, then what to theatricalize, or dramatize presently?

It seems to me that Synge's theatre presents aesthetically a prophetic answer, by anticipation, to such questions; the Symbolist elements are an attempt to make some sense of the Naturalist framework, this by de-politicizing it—or relocating the "classless society" not in the future but in the "revolutionary" past of fate and tragic destiny and inevitability, one that has been and will come again, and that bonds, unifies and links all of suffering humanity more surely than any mere surface changes, having to do with reallocation of resources, or living a little longer or less so, can do...

Coincidentally, one of the 'classics' of theatrical Naturalism, maybe its formal creator (with the preface to *Miss Julie*, 1888), August Strindberg followed a similar itinerary, as did André Antoine, whose Naturalist Théatre Libre yielded to a theatre he later directed that featured Symbolist works. Yet, for both Strindberg and Antoine the evolution was sequential, the Symbolist period following that of Naturalism, surely for many of the reasons limned above, whereas it is the strange originality and uniqueness of Synge's theatre, on the other hand, to combine, fuse and merge these two styles—as if to attempt to construct the cathedral of eternity on the shifting sands of matter, so that what we have described as his Symbolist Naturalism or Naturalist Symbolism might be better named a Cosmic, or even Mystical Naturalism, or a theatrical "mysticism-without-God", even a "natural supernaturalism".[8]

Such a turning in theatre and culture, of course, raises as many, if not many more questions than it answers, not only in terms of Naturalism, whose basic tenets, which as I hope we've shown involve political upheaval and revolution (whether implicitly violent, as with Hauptmann and Gorky, or more patiently pacifist, as with Shaw), it very much modifies, even subverts, but also in terms of the very Symbolist aesthetics it weds to the Naturalistic framework by the fiat of dazzling dramatic genius and commitment. There are clear limits, for example, to the extent that the attitude, situation and predicament of the Aran Islanders, or Irish country folk in their present incarnations or even medieval avatars, can serve as an incarnation of the universal human condition. Insofar as there is a politics to Synge's theatre it would seem to apply to a humanity for whom ethnicity (either Irish, or, by extension, some other) comprised much of what makes sense of life. While Synge's version of ethnicity is wise and philosophical, compassionate and lyrical, it is surely very much of an aesthetic version or rendition, doubtless containing a high proportion of imagination and the sort of wish-fulfillment that, for Freud, made the creations of the artist very comparable to dreaming. Alas, in recent years and decades, we've seen how the invention of a "return to roots" is also likely to reawaken or even create an all-too-actual atavism, cruelty, prejudice, and to be harmonious with, even invoked as justification of genocidal behavior and attitudes.

In conclusion, it should be observed that Synge's theatre—through its manifest recourse to the arsenal of Symbolist aesthetics and folk "costumery", and in its refusal to cater to a debased preference for happy endings and optimistic visions of society and culture in a time when the revolutionary promises and the premises that had been propelling it were increasingly revealed as accompanied by a formerly underestimated coefficient of uncertainty—solved certain questions for Naturalism. These were, namely, how to preserve the clear advances and progress of that style—its immediacy and provocation, honesty and authenticity, its assaults on the stage/audience separations and its relevance to a wider public than merely an elite seeking diversion or distraction. Yet these answers, as all answers do, come with a price: in Synge's case a proletarian universalism, looming, outraged, impending, acted and acted out by Naturalism, from Zola, with ever increasing urgency, until the firebrand Gorky (in and out of the Tsar's prisons), was exchanged against a philosophical one, anchored in a pre-Christian pagan (largely) invented ethnicity, couched in the language and dialect (Synge's own!) of fate, resignation, ritual and commemoration, basically saying, like music (and Synge's theater is nothing if not musical)[9] can so well: "it has always been so". Ultimately, since it's a narrowing of existence to say that it can or must be lived only in the perspective of its last moments, or even 'limit situations', what Synge is doing here is making a (lay) religion and philosophy out of art, which, however consoling, fails to address some of the pressing questions for a wider humanity that Naturalism had been raising: yes, death is what we all wait for, of others and ourselves, but, what with "death at an early age", chances are the ruling classes will wait so much longer for it. Meanwhile, the oppressed of this world, so bamboozled and benumbed by prevailing power relations are they that their very deaths are stolen from them in a cacophony of media and every other kind of commercial and exploitative assault on consciousness. The poor die, nothing new, in the rich man's war.

Therefore I think it makes sense to regard what is being offered here, in Synge's *Riders* particularly and his theatre generally (as in that of the "Irish Revival", and perhaps other ethnic movements)—aesthetically, culturally, and in a way, even politically—as a rare, if ineluctable moment of synthesis, in the Hegelian sense of a point that will be and must be transcended, bypassed and 'overcome'. Rebellion (Cain's, for example), after all, is a law as ancient as renunciation, and, just possibly, more honorable, and, ultimately, with so much more to offer. After all, assuming we 'bet' on upsetting things, twisting Pascal's famous logic[10] a bit: what have we to lose, even if we're wrong?

# IX. Living History: *Chicken Soup With Barley*

In Arnold Wesker's *Chicken Soup With Barley* (1958) the players represent roles that are embedded in a specific historical and political context and environment, that of England of the twenty tumultuous years between 1936 and 1956. In no other play in the Naturalist parade we have been reviewing is the connection to reality so tightly empirical, political and factual. Hauptmann's *Weavers*, so successfully and significantly performed at André Antoine's Théatre Libre, in 1892, was very flagrantly a recreation of a watershed worker's rebellion of 50 years earlier, the one that constituted an epiphany for Marx and Engels, in the revelation that the proletariat did not have to (wait to) be guided toward revolution, from 'above', as the Bruno Bauer and Young Hegelians had been insisting, but, as the class that 'had nothing to lose but its chains', was ideally placed to liberate itself—in fact such a 'class war' could be waged and won in no other way.

Hauptmann's play, however, comes at a remove of half-a-century from the events it dramatizes and is certainly as much, if not more, about the cultural and political context in which it was performed about halfway between the Civil War in France (Marx called it that, in his book about the rise and fall of the 'revolutionary' Paris Commune of 1870-71, *The Civil War in France*) and the Russian Revolution as it was about the age in which it was set. Also, it covers only those events, the Silesian Weaver's strike and rebellion of 1844, and their immediate aftermath—conveyed, therefore, with something like an Aristotelian tragic intensity—because the represented time and the relatively short historical time very nearly coincide. Essentially *The Weavers* starts with scenes depicting the motivation for the action (inhumanity of capital, through its representatives), followed by the workers' attack on property and the very principle of ownership (according to Engel's 'reporting' on the events) on which it is based, then ending just as the workers are about to face an army counterattack. Also distancing is the fact that the weavers are patently not of a theatre-going class, and would be relatively foreign, even exotic entities in the eyes of a sophisticated Parisian audience of the 1890's.

Not so for the people in Wesker's play, working class also—but from the East End of one of the world's great cities, and ethnically, if in a secular way, Jewish also, thereby *a fortiori* a literate, even educated and class-conscious group. Additionally, the history that the play is structured around is identical to that through which its audience, and/or its parents and older friends and acquaintances have been and are still living through. The world and time of the first act, set in East End, London, in 1936, is one that is molten and in process of formation, where we tune into the British working class at a time seemingly of limitless possibility and promise. That same organic connection between Judaism and Bolshevism that was a significant factor in the Russian Revolution of October 1917, is very much in place here. The Spanish Civil War, a few months old, is an important historical context as well, since one of the major characters is about to volunteer to fight on the republican side against the fascists. This is Dave, fiancée of the daughter, Ada, of the couple formed by Harry and Sarah Kahn.   October 4, 1936, time indicated for opening of scene 1 of Act I, is obviously the date of the anti-Moseley riot, Oswald Moseley being the British, pro-Nazi fascist who was planning to lead his followers on a (legally protected) march through Jewish (yet) working class East End; so Jewish working-class objectors to this march found themselves fighting pitched (bottles and rocks against billy clubs) battles with the police who were protecting the civil rights of the fascist demonstrators.  These 'battles' take place, as in *The Weavers*, off stage, between scenes, with bleeding and otherwise traumatized workers' casualties then appearing on stage fresh from the action.

This aspect of 'absolute realism' might qualify the play as the culmination of Zola's ambition, expressed in *Le Naturalisme au théâtre*, of breaking down the separation between theatre and reality, stage and audience!  Similarly Wesker, wanting to emphasize that no exit would be permitted from the stage of this world indeed announced in a "NOTE TO ACTORS AND PRODUCERS": "My people are not caricatures. They are real (though fiction), and if they are portrayed as caricatures the point of all these plays will be lost."[1]   A few lines later when Wesker says "I am at one with these people", he can't be accused of exaggerating or 'dramatizing', since he's made no secret, in interviews and other statements, that his characters are more or less composite portraits created from those he has known, especially his family; a very good example of this is his mother Leah Wesker, rendered certainly as Sarah Kahn in the trilogy.[2]

Characters are of course individualized clearly by the nature of their response to events, but they take on depth and coherence only against their background and context, changing, often like chameleons according to the changing nature of the times.  In fact changes in what the characters say and think are due solely to the differing perspectives afforded by a developing world situation and by an altered life-style for the proletarian class in question: Sarah's socialist credo, which she shares with just about everybody else at the play's inception, in 1936, has become a rare act of stubborn tenacious faith by its conclusion (or after the Soviet invasion of Hungary). Strangely, she appeals to her disillusioned son at the end of the play to be allowed to hold on to her beliefs, not for their cogency but because she needs desperately something to believe in!:

> SARAH
> (*exasperated*). All right then! Nothing, then! It all comes down to nothing....
> Please, Ronnie, don't let me finish this life thinking I lived for nothing.[3]

Wesker's characters represent not so much individuals, real as he insists they are, but a range of possible adaptations to an external situation—birth, of course, setting the model for all succeeding ones over which we'll have no control. Individuality, far from being freely chosen and created by each, has been assigned us as a fate. It becomes, as for one of Wesker's characters in a later play, irrelevant to talk about, nowadays when only the group matters:

> I don't see the point of insisting you're an individual—you're born one anyway....
> But [what matters is] a group together, depending on each other, knowing what they
> want, knowing how to get it.[4]

The stage itself, in Wesker's theatre, tends to lack particularity and individuality: either institutional and therefore interchangeable (kitchen, army barracks, union halls), or as in the home setting for *Chicken Soup*, just a typical working class London home, the one a family with a certain income can afford. An exception to this rule of interchangeability might be the country setting in *I'm Talking About Jerusalem*, of 1960, where the Kahn's daughter, Ada, and her husband, David, back from the wars against fascism (Spanish Civil and World War II), have moved to escape the alienating evils of the city; however this experiment with 'individual rebellion' significantly turns out to be a failure, with the couple winding up back in London.

So as far as Naturalism in theatre is concerned, we're crossing a few thresholds here: not only is the historical, social, cultural and political context right out of the papers as we've been reading them "all these years"; but the very people on stage are very nearly the Weskers, who've been living next door—until they moved away to slightly better quarters (we know because we've followed them there). Something about this style must foretell also the realer-than-real, the hyperreal, the virtual reality of the derealizing French theorist, Jean Baudrillard; although his ideas will be in even better harmony with the theatre of David Storey, treated later, where reality is not merely resembled and represented but positively duplicated and acted out on stage. On a less exalted level, we recognize here the flat parody and mockery of reality in today's enormously popular reality shows on TV, as well as in visits to internet webcam sites where we see and hear people going about their (formerly private) 'business'. Or to take a more Nietzschean turn, when you 'realize the real', you're begging the question that the real is not already (some kind of) illusion—that what you're representing is the real.

Undeniably, of course, Wesker is working out of some of the core elements of the Naturalist tradition in theatre, as in literature generally; for him, as for Zola, Ibsen, Strindberg and Gorky, man is very much a creature of emotional and especially biological needs, demands and urges. Food, for instance is a fundamental factor, metaphorically and literally and in every other conceivable way in his theatre, as is apparent from the very names of his works; from his play *The Kitchen*, set there, through *Chicken Soup With Barley* to *Chips With Everything*. At the other end of the digestive process, shit is a key dramatic factor in *Chicken Soup*; in Strindberg's *Miss Julie*, there were, it will be remembered, some very important fecal reminiscences, when Jean is recalling to the enthralled Julie, how he got a look at her with her panties down when crawling through the waste-soaked straw of an outhouse. In *Chicken Soup With Barley*, the shit is not only recalled it has, so to speak, hit the fan. Here Harry Kahn, erstwhile reluctant demonstrator, of Act I, set in 1936, who talked more radical than he acted, then malingering father of the family, of Act II, set in 1946-47, when employment has replaced revolution as proletarian priority, and who has had few strokes by Scene 1 of Act III, set in 1955; or after another decade of entropy, when a kind of social amnesia has set in, whereby the working class seems to be eager to forget entirely it ever dreamt of revolution, he loses, *on stage*, control over his bowels, in front of company, yet:

> (HARRY *wakes up with a jerk. Something has happened. He tries hurriedly to rise.*)
> HARRY
> Sarah, quick, help me.
> SARAH
> What! It's happened? *(She moves quickly to him)*
> MONTY
> What is it, Harry boy?
> SARAH
> It's happened, Harry? Well, quickly, then, quickly.
> (HARRY, *crippled by paralysis and this attack of incontinence, shuffles, painfully towards the toilet, with* SARAH *almost dragging him along. He whines and groans pathetically.*)
> HARRY
> In front of Monty and Bessie. I'm so ashamed.[5]

Whatever Wesker thought he was saying thereby, this 'accident' surely conveys historical devolution through biological decline—for Harry's pathetic condition is inescapably a metaphor for the predicament of the English proletariat: just as history has passed out of its control, so has Harry lost control of his very bodily functions.

However, Wesker is not only the Naturalist of food and shit. He likes to take a good look, in his theatre at something most of us spend our whole lives trying to ignore: the fact of death and dying. A later play, *The Friends*, of 1970, is a kind of social phenomenology of death. In this connection we might recall the death of poor Anna in Gorky's *Lower Depths*, a world where people have ceased to be able to afford privacy, so one where everything, even dying takes place in public and is preeminently a social fact, even in Pierre Bourdieu's sense of a social death (isolation etc.) that is a preliminary to the physical one. Wesker's focus is social too, but here there is no "social death", rather the character becomes all the more important, with everyone hanging on her every word and motion, as the end nears. *The Friends* is about the challenge a death represents, for the dying person and even more so for those 'left behind' to try to make some sense out of the life and lives that have been lived. Here friends, associates, a lover and a brother gather round the bed of the central character Esther, who is moribund, although quite articulate all through Act I, at the end of which she dies; through all of the second and final act she lies 'dead' on stage, under a sheet, occasionally lifted while a point someone is making is thereby emphasized.[6] Especially this act, with the 'unreality' of Esther's body lying on stage throughout, would relate rather to some kind of theatrical formalism, or even neo-Maeterlinckian symbolism. By 1970, time of the production of this play, Wesker's theatre has passed out of the realm of Naturalism, strictly speaking, at least as far as we've been defining it, in terms of its connection to proletarian consciousness and radical politics. Death here is a private matter, up to the moribund and her friends to interpret and accept as best as they can, not something that represents, as it certainly does for the paralysis of Harry Kahn in *Chicken Soup*, the decline of a whole class.

Whether through illness (Harry's in *Chicken Soup*), and its most embarrassing concomitant, incontinence, or by way of vivid representation of the physical and social realities of death and aging in modern times (*The Friends, The Old Ones*), Wesker's dramatic imagination is symbolic and metaphorical as well as naturalistic, literal and material. From this 'signifying' point of view the two most radical moments in his theatre would be the Act I of *Chicken Soup*, set in October 1936, in the midst and as a backdrop of the anti-Moseley demonstrations/riots/protests, at a time when the Spanish Civil War (beginning in July of 1936) was constituting a call to arms in the struggle against fascism by the forces of social progress; and also the blatantly anarchist-communist dénouement of an earlier play *The Kitchen* (1959), with Peter, the cook-worker, unhappy with the irrationality and injustice of the whole (capitalist) system, rather than just with his place in it, sabotaging the oven, thereby destroying the whole enterprise. Peter here is playing the proletariat, who as Marx predicted early on, would be impossible to "pay off", buy off or co-opt: "No quantitative relief of its poverty, no illusory hierarchical incorporation, can supply a lasting cure for its dissatisfaction"[7] Like the Silesian workers in *The Weavers*, Peter clearly represents the kind of proletariat who has no respect for whatever rewards the boss has to offer. That Peter's resistance, one that has erupted as a 'return of the repressed' from the depths of what must be some kind of proletarian collective unconscious, is a matter of principle, not pay or working conditions, is clear from the restaurant owner's puzzled lamentation-appeal to the 'saboteur' that closes that play, end of story:

> MARANGO
>     (*turning to* FRANK [another cook, one not so unhappy as Peter, for instance enjoying a prerogative of his 'position' to feel up the waitresses] *and making a gentle appeal*). Why does everybody sabotage me, Frank? I give work, I pay well, yes? They eat what they want, don't they? I don't know what more to give a man. He works, he eats, I give him money. This is life, isn't it? I haven't made a mistake, have I? I live in the right world, don't I? (*to* PETER) And you've stopped this world....You've stopped it. Well why? Maybe you can tell me something I don't know—just tell me. (*No answer.*) I want to learn something. (*to the kitchen*) Is there something I don't know? (PETER *rises and in pain* [has injured himself wrecking the kitchen] *moves off. When he reaches a point back center stage* MARANGO *cries at him.*) BLOODY FOOL! (*Rushes round to him.*) What more do you want? What is there more, tell me? (*He shakes Peter, but gets no reply.* PETER *again tries to leave. Again* MARANGO *cries out.*) What is there more? (PETER *stops, turns in pain and sadness, shakes his head as if to say—'if you don't know, I cannot explain'. And so he moves right off stage.* MARANGO *is left facing his staff, who stand around, almost accusingly, looking at him. And he asks again—*) What is there more? What is there more? What is there more?[8]

This nothing-if-not revolutionary mood in Wesker's earliest theatre,[9] burning so brightly here proved to be short-lived, since the only thing, in his later production, that comes anywhere near matching its ultimate and defining vision of the worker as Samson who brings down the Temple of the Philistine-Capitalists, rather than live on in proletarian sub-humanity, are the protest/riots of Act I in *Chicken Soup* when the Jewish East End workers rushed out to battle against the forces of fascist reaction.[10] However, with Act II of *Chicken Soup*, set after the war, in 1946-47 we have landed squarely in the Brave New World of accommodation, adjustment, compromise and reform:

> *The Kahns have moved to an L.C.C. block of flats in Hackney—the 1930 kind, with railings. The working class is a little more respectable now, they have not long since voted in a Labour government.* [stage directions, beginning of Act]

Harry, surely emblematic of the evolution (or devolution) of the British working class is now *shirking* work rather than *pretending* to demonstrate:

During the Moseley riots of Act I, in the radical year of 1936 he wound up running off to his mother's to drink tea and read a book when things took a violent turn on the street, crowing nevertheless, in the timeless tradition of Falstaff "We won! Boys, we won the day" when it was safe to come out! The climate in 1946-47 is no longer that of revolution, of overturning or even subverting The System, but rising within it. Labour has come to power through the ballot box, not on the battlefield, so will be working within the law.

The Kahn's daughter Ada and her husband Dave, just returned from the war, are making their ill-fated individualist plans to escape to the country, subject of the sequel play, *I'm Talking About Jerusalem* (1960). Ronnie Kahn, their son who was 5 in Act I of *Chicken Soup* and now 15 in June 1946, when the opening scene of Act II is set, has of course become politically conscious and is trying to be the radical his father never really amounted to. Fifteen months later, in the next scene of Act II, Ronnie is describing himself as a socialist poet and is working in a bookstore; but his conversations with his supposedly still radical mother, Sarah, rather turn on getting a pay raise than disseminating revolutionary propaganda. Likewise the leitmotif of Sarah's communication with her husband no longer is the man's political timidity, but rather his inability or unwillingness to hold onto a job. By the beginning of Act III, set in 1955, any kind of socialist or communist dream has become totally impracticable, except perhaps as material for Sarah Kahn's "feel-good" personal fantasy. Enter a friend, Monty, who was at the very center of the worker's turmoil in 1936, with his pregnant wife Bessie, who threatens to leave if politics comes up; as a matter of fact, Monty has already left the (Communist) Party, while Bessie's only hope is that no one ever know he was ever a member, in fact that not even Monty remember!:

> BESSIE
> Listen, Sarah. Monty's got a nice little greengrocer's business in Manchester, no one knows he was ever a member of the Party and we're all happy. It's better he forgets it.[11]

A key reason for his disillusion, as a matter of fact the first one he mentions, was Stalin's (in)famous liquidation of the Jewish Anti-Fascist Committee after the war, which brought an end to a symbiotic connection between Judaism and Communism that not even the brutal purges of the late 30's were able to sever[12]:

> MONTY
> Listen, Sarah. Remember Spain? Remember how we were proud of Dave and the other boys who answered the call? But did Dave ever tell you the way some of the Party members refused to fight alongside the Trotskyists? And one or two of the Trotskyists didn't come back and they weren't killed in the fighting either? And

remember Itzack Pheffer—the Soviet Yiddish writer? We used to laugh because Itzack Pheffer was a funny name—ha, ha. Where's Itzack Pheffer? everyone used to say. Well, we know now, don't we. The great 'leader' is dead now, and we know. The whole committee of the Jewish Anti-Fascist League were shot! Shot, Sarah! In our land of socialism. That was *our* land—what a land that was for us![13]

Monty then goes on to announce his and of course his whole generation's massive return to 'private life':

I just make a comfortable living and I'm happy. Bessie—bless her—is having a baby. (*Taps* BESSIE'S *belly*). I'm going to give him all that I can, pay for his education, university if he likes, and then I shall be satisfied. A man can't do anything more, Sarah, believe me. There's nothing more to life than a house, some friends and a family—take my word.[14]

The next (and last scene) of the last act of the play, which skips another year or so, to December of 1956, or right after the Russian invasion of Hungary, is pervaded by a profound sense of disillusionment, hopelessness, meaninglessness and absurdity. The same characters who we had seen rushing out into the street to fight the fascists and the police twenty years earlier are now sitting around playing cards, which is how the scene opens. This is a world of anonymity, reification and alienation, where Television is king. Events no longer take place in the political realm of possibility but in the screened worlds of illusion and delusion. Sarah, for instance, returning from a visit to a noisy neighbors flat reassures her cardplaying circle that the disturbance was over nothing!:

Children! They don't know what to do with themselves. Seems she'd just spent the evening watching television with Philip and it was a horror film or something and he kept frightening her...[15]

Enter Ronnie (an obvious stand-in for Wesker himself), fresh from a disillusioning time working in the kitchen of a restaurant in Paris[16], where he found no proletarian glory in fashioning the new man and the new society, just a lot of frightened people who can't think of anything else to do with themselves: "That's all we are—people terrified of old age, hoping for the football pools...". This, combined with the murder of the Jewish Anti-Fascist Committee and invasion of Hungary has meant "I've lost my faith and I've lost my ambition."

Between this sad dénouement and the postwar epoch of the previous act of this play, Ronnie however had been busy with a little bit of progressive proselytism of the romantic sort, a 'missionary' adventure whose dramatic expression for Wesker was the curious play *Roots* (1959), produced the year after *Chicken Soup*, and set in an atmosphere and place of simple country folk, nearly as raw as the 'naked' Aran islands where Synge set his *Riders to the Sea*.

*Roots* is set in "an isolated cottage in Norfolk, the house of the Bealeses." Strangely, Ronnie who catalyzes the action here is absent from the stage, talked about, argued and obsessed over, yes, but just not there, not physically anyway. The central role of this play belongs to a Beatie Bryant, 22 year old sister of Jenny Beales, wife in turn of a Jimmy Beales—hard working, uneducated country folk. Beatie has fallen for the radical and progressive Ronnie, when she was working in a restaurant in a big city, where he was doing his proletarian bit in the kitchen. In fact she has been playing Galatea to his Pygmalion, who has been raising her consciousness in all sorts of ways—not only politically: she has started to paint, be interested in politics and ideas, and has brought the good news home, where she has been telling her country people all about a world they knew nothing of: Every other word out of her mouth is "Ronnie says". She really expects he will marry her, and as a matter of fact expects his arrival, all during the play, at the cottage in Norfolk; but instead of showing up Ronnie sends her a letter announcing his decision to break up the relationship:

> 'My dear Beatie. It wouldn't really work would it? My ideas about handing on a new kind of life are quite useless and romantic if I'm really honest. If I were a healthy human being it might have been all right but most of us intellectuals are pretty sick and neurotic...and we couldn't build a world even if we were given the reins of government...'[17]

Thereby he admits to the same kind of powerlessness, on a romantic level, that his father, Harry and, symbolically the international proletariat had been admitting to, on a political level, of realizing their dreams for a better world. Symptomatically Ronnie's 'determinism' shows he is as much in need of an education as the 'student' he has been helping. So let's return him to an important page in Marx we've cited before he might have forgotten or overlooked:

> The materialist doctrine that men are products of circumstances and upbringing, and that, therefore, changed men are products of other circumstances and changed upbringing, forgets that it is men that change circumstances, and that the educator himself needs educating.[18]

It's telling also that Ronnie has talked about being "given the reins of government", not taking them, as if ruling classes ever give up their sway voluntarily. As a matter of fact, this can prompt some wonder as to whether the elected postwar government of the Labour Party in England represented progress on the part of its proletariat in achieving its dream of a classless society and a better world, or rather, effectively, a reformist cutoff and short circuit of its ideals.

A few years later than *Roots*, with *Chips With Everything* (1962), a play set in the grim reality of the British military, we find Wesker still focused on this fascinating, but ultimately frustrating theme of breaking down the barriers between the classes. Here the central role is that of a Pip Thomson, who, although from the upper strata of society, has decided on the practically unprecedented course of remaining a mere conscript, instead of going to officer school. This choice is of course enormously threatening to the military hierarchy, which exerts all kinds of pressures to get him to change his mind. At first he is successful in his resistance, but ultimately he yields, in a crucially disappointing if credible dénouement. What causes him ultimately to "break" is the insight that a harassing "pilot officer" stumbles upon that Pip's motives have more to do with Nietzsche than Marx or Jesus:

PILOT OFFICER
        We know, you and I, don't we? Comradeship? Not that, not because of the affinity of one human being to another, not that. Guilt? Shame because of your fellow beings' suffering? You don't feel that either. Not guilt. An inferiority complex, a feeling of modesty? My God. Not that either. There's nothing humble about you, is there? Thompson, you wanted to do more than simply share the joy of imparting knowledge to your friends; no, not modesty. Not that. What then? What if not those things, my lad? You and I? Shall I say it? Shall I? Power. Power, isn't it. Among your own people there were too many who were powerful, the competition was too great, but here, among lesser men—here among the yobs, among the good-natured yobs, you could be king. KING. Supreme and all powerful, eh? Well? Not true? Deny it—deny it, then. We know—you and I—we know, Thompson.
PIP
        Oh, God—
PILOT OFFICER
        God? God? Why do you call upon God? Are you his son? Better still, then. You are found out even more, illusions of grandeur, Thompson. We know that also, that's what we know, that's what we have, the picture you have of yourself, and now that we know that, you're really finished, destroyed. You're destroyed, Thompson. No man survives whose motive is discovered, no man. Messiah to the masses![19]

One could reply to this kind of psychological onslaught, of course, with something like the familiar Hegelian argument that History with a large H is made out of history with a small h: that is its cunning; the motives that get us and things moving are always base, lustful, greedy, vain, self-serving and egotistic... However, Pip has already been weakened by the inability, surely the structural incapacity of his class, to establish a connection of real solidarity with "the common man". Chas, a fellow conscript who was trying to be Pip's friend, sums up the falsity of the latter's patronizing position with surgical precision late in the play, significantly rejecting the first person plural Pip uses to refer to "us" as opposed to the officers:

PIP
        We'll do anything they [upper classes] want just because they know how to smile at us.

CHAS
      You mean *I'll* do what they want, not you boy. You're one of them—you're
just playing games with 'em, and us mugs is in the middle—[20]

It's no surprise, then, that *Chips*, in 1962, with the divorce symbolically
pronounced as "final" between the ruling and the lower classes, represents
just about the end of the Naturalist adventure in Wesker's theatre, although
he continued and continues to write,[21] and profusely, inspired by other
traditions—humanist, individualist, ethical—even a kind of rediscovery of
his Jewish roots and values.[22]

    It seems to me that of the four other plays I'm considering as Naturalist,
starting with the clarion call that is *The Kitchen*, of 1958, *Roots*, of 1959, and
*I'm Talking About Jerusalem*, of 1960, *Chicken Soup With Barley*, of 1959,
would be the central dramatic statement, or at least the broadest one,
covering at it does such a grand sweep of time, from England of the thirties
to the middle fifties. *The Kitchen*, ending with the destruction of the oven in
which the 'old world' did its cooking,[23] would amount to a declaration of the
war between the classes, in so many words, a revolution—which we see very
much on the march in the proletarian anti-fascist street demonstrations and
riots of Act I of *Chicken Soup*. Subsequently, *Roots*, *I'm Talking About
Jerusalem* and *Chips* will incarnate various individualist attempts of halting
the devolution of the working class and the collapse of its dreams of a better
world; resulting, emblematically, in *fiasco*, as dramatized so brilliantly and
exhaustively in the ensuing Acts II and III (1940's and 50's) of *Chicken
Soup*, with their sad tale of the entropy and cooptation of The British
Working Class, after their proud moment in the sun of Act I (1930's)

    Symptomatically I think, it's a fact that hope for social change is
presented in the plays after *Chicken Soup* as being dashed by either (1) the
fiasco of the illusions of individuality and personal solutions to social
problems; as in the escape of Ann and Dave to the country at the beginning
of *I'm Talking About Jerusalem*, who return to the city, after the collapse of
their hopes, at the end of the play; or (2) in the aporia and ineluctable failure
of "revolution from above", as in *Roots* and *Chips*, whether catalyzed, in
*Roots*, by the Pygmalion of a "socialist poet", Ronnie Kahn, who's seduced
his Galatea of a country working class woman, then abandoned her; or in
*Chips*, by the upper class Pip who after flirting with the idea of solidarity
with the lower class of conscripts, is drawn through the pressure of relentless
social and psychological forces back into his class of provenance and on to
officer school.

# X.   Living Theatre: *The Brig*

"Sans la prison, nous saurions que nous sommes tous déjà en prison"

—Blanchot

If ever a play pretended not to be "just a play" this would be *The Brig*, Kenneth H. Brown's "creation"[1] of 1963, become a watershed production for The Living Theatre of Julian Beck and Judith Malina (Julian designed the set, Judith directed the play) for the stormy season of 1964, ending in the closing of the theatre by the Internal Revenue Service, after a sort of siege, followed by the flight of The Living Theatre to a lengthy period of European exile.  Set in a U.S. Marines military jail in Japan in 1957, and based on a 30 day sentence the author says he served out there (Schechner 212-13), ostensibly for the offense of coming back late to the barracks, the stage was designed as what the audience is very obviously supposed to understand as an exact replica of a military brig as is possible to create.  The prisoners are kept in a large pen where basically they sleep in bunks; the holding-sleeping pen is surrounded by a walkway where guards are stationed, each on their own 'territory', defined and delimited by a white line, to cross which the prisoner must ask and secure permission from the guard concerned.  The prisoners come out and circulate for various reasons, to go to the head, be searched or for roll call, or to be lectured, berated, humiliated and even 'beaten' (basically blows to the stomach with a billy club).  Every few feet, as the prisoner enters another guard's domain he must request again permission to cross, in a certain preset formula of a phrase that must be shouted at the top of his lungs; the guard as often as not answering "I can't hear you", as loudly as the prisoner has been shouting, so the prisoner must shout even louder, inconceivably, ridiculously loud.

No, this is not a user-friendly production, this!  Prisoners are called by number, not name.  The only time they are allowed to talk to each other, in fact, is when there is a new arrival, who is told in detail about the rules and regulations, after having been rudely oriented in general by one of the guards.  The goal of this and other humiliations and regimentations, what with every moment of the prisoner's time, each of his actions being precisely scripted and programmed, calibrated and formalized, is to condition marines who have been guilty, it seems, for swervings, for the most part surely quite anodyne, from the military program, to become absolutely obedient automatons, alienated, smooth-running killing machines.

As a matter of fact, Arnold Wesker used a similar setting, a British military barracks, for the brutally realistic environment of *Chips With Everything* (1962) of about a year earlier, so we have a case either of direct impact or that of a shared cultural climate of resistance to a "society of regimentation", most nakedly visible in the military sector.[2] Another play by Wesker that seems even more likely to have influenced Brown's approach would have been *The Kitchen*, of 1959, when it was produced memorably and appreciated enthusiastically in New York City.[3] As for *Chips With Everything* and *The Brig*, the setting of *The Kitchen* was designed as a replica of "the real thing", where what is being enacted is a "day in the life" of those who work there; but Brown's play is one giant step beyond Wesker's naturalism, however faithful. Although dehumanized, alienated, manipulated and exploited, the people in Wesker's plays generally, whether military, culinary, East End or country proletarian or lumpenprole, still had names, were situated in micro-narratives of love, friendship and family relations, as well as macro-narratives of class solidarity (or fragmentation), revolution and cultural identity, loss or mourning thereof. They are human beings with distinct individualities and identities, even if failed or disappointed ones; not so here, in *The Brig*, where the prisoners are all numbers, except for a brief moment when, very much against the rules, Prisoner Six, breaking down, utters his own name, and is addressed as such by the guard (the guards, significantly, *do* have names, this one called, ironically, Grace!):

SIX
     [*from his cell*]. My name is not Six. It's James Turner. Let me out of here....
     *Two men in white coats and trousers carrying a stretcher and a strait jacket enter and are led to the cell of Six. They enter it.*
SIX
     What the hell is going on here? Leave me alone.
GRACE
     Just relax, James Turner. You are getting out of here. (Brown 1963: 73)

But Grace is being personal only to pacify the prisoner while he's being strapped to the stretcher:

     *The two men come out of the cell carrying a stretcher with the prisoner on it secured to the stretcher in the strait jacket.*
     *The prisoner babbles as they carry him off. (ibid, 1963: 73)*

Wesker's plays had narrative story lines, this being the case also for the entire 'tradition' of naturalistic theatre, setting clear, seemingly inviolable and ineluctable limits to Zola's catalytic ambition of breaking down the separations between drama and 'real life'. Not as if it is absolutely unquestionable, as writing fanatics, enthusiastic teachers, and other "content providers" whose bread is buttered on the side of story insist, that there is something about reality that is intrinsically narrative, which of course it (at least very often) isn't[4], just that it has been impossible or inconceivable to represent reality without turning it into some kind of story. This has been that last shred of a fence between theatre and life. Both *Chips* and *The Kitchen*, for instance, very much in the tradition of the Zola idea of art as the mirror-on-the-side-of-the road which necessarily reflects the gutter, however had narrative story lines—that qualify and theatralize any raw reality they depict; after all, not every military unit is favored, as in *Chips*, with the dramatic presence of an upper class private-by-choice trying to be chummy with "the common man", nor does every kitchen harbor an iconoclastic cook, one with communist-anarchist leanings or tendencies, who after an affair with a waitress turns sour, turns the righteous wrath of his revolutionary-proletarian class toward the destruction of the whole restaurant. In other words, enlivening and flavoring Wesker's faithful depiction of reality is a good dose of artifice, idealism and maybe just plain wishful thinking. Both *Chips* and *The Kitchen* not only had clear story-lines, the reluctant officer for the former, the disappointed cook-lover for the latter—but also a recognizably theatrical framework and structure, complete with rising action and peripety: the death of a persecuted private, intensifying the protagonist's conflict in *Chips*; in *The Kitchen*, the decision of his mistress to stay with her husband, who has bribed her with the offer of a new house, that forces the cook to realize that the whole world of private property in which that calculating decision was made, incarnated by this kitchen, must be abolished if there is to be any hope for him and his proletarian class. Then there's the eternally dramatic moment of recognition, either of something true about the universe or a dropping of the veil of illusion about oneself and others: say the boss's enlightenment in *The Kitchen*, when he realizes the nature of the cook's dissatisfaction, too structural and total to be bought off by anything the system has to offer; or the scene, in Wesker's *Roots* (1959), when the country-lass, Beatie Bryant, receives the news in a letter from her radical-intellectual lover, Ronnie Kahn, that he is dumping her, which shows her, and us, that education- from-above (à la Pygmalion) has its limits. Likewise, there is always a dénouement in Wesker's plays, arising of course out of this very moment of recognition or disillusionment, a beginning-over-again, if only looked forward to as starting after the curtain falls, when we'll 'know better' than before it went up. This is the case in the tradition of theatre generally, which, even at its saddest, teaches sobering lessons of the sort of "call no day happy until it's over" from *Oedipus*—through the lessons

Shakespeare teaches about the anarchy and unpredictability of the human heart in great tragedies that seem to occur in some wondrous domain beyond good and evil, like *Macbeth, Hamlet* and *Lear*; to the naturalist genre where the lessons *represented* seem all to be about the ways physical, psychological and political life are culturally and biologically predetermined, with an occasional flash, usually quickly dampened, if always left somewhat smoldering, of human liberty.

*The Brig,* however, certainly presents itself as having moved beyond merely *representing* reality to *duplicating* it, just as if, if a Frederick Wiseman had been allowed to film 16 hours in the life of a military jail, this play would have been supererogatory. All the same, even for the most faithful of documentaries, or documentary-type productions, a certain amount of art and artifice, as well as selectivity, ineluctably seems to surface. Those 16 hours pass, as far as the audience is concerned, in a lot less than two, however raucous and harrowing[5] Certain activities "more equal than others" are very obviously chosen for their dramatic impact and representability; we do not watch the prisoners eat or write letters, for instance; instead we are told they have, but we do see them, in an absolute frenzy of mad meaningless activity, make their jail as spotless as a hospital operating room:

> ...*Water from the large garbage can and soapsuds veritably flood the deck, with those on their knees scrubbing and getting soaking wet. The squeegee man fights desperately to keep the soap forward of the scrubbers, and the swabbers dry up the water as quickly as possible, rinsing the water in their buckets. The window washer wipes the windows one at a time with a wet rag and then rubs them dry feverishly, for what seems much longer than is necessary, and the guards from their safe and dry positions issue many warnings and instructions.* (Brown 66)

This, together with the breakdown of Prisoner Six, constitute two very dramatic and privileged moments that stand out, even traumatically so, in the enactment of this extraordinary ordinary reality of military incarceration. Another moment, perhaps most horrifying of all, since it hits its audience when it's just getting settled in its seats, occurs about two minutes from the play's beginning, is the shock of witnessing a guard, gratuitously and outrageously, striking a new prisoner, and more than once, in what one must gather is the *customary* initiation to this brig of terror:

TEPPERMAN
    [*hitting the prisoner in the stomach repeatedly with his billy*]. I am going to be watching you among the rest of my lice, and if you are not squared away...[*Pauses, then smiling.*] I will clean up the deck with you. Is that clear. Two?
TWO
    [*doubling over from the blows*]. Yes, sir. (Brown 50)

Among the peripeties that life has to offer perhaps none is as disappointing, and memorably so, than to witness (or experience) a passively suffered beating. Surely, we will all remember, and for the rest of our lives, as long as our minds can function at all, the first time we saw something like this happen, and *a fortiori* if the beaten is ourselves or someone we love and admire and may have looked to, in fact, for shelter and protection from exactly such contingencies.[6] The cruelty, or indifference, as Camus' 'absurd' would have it, of the universe to human need or desire is one thing, difficult enough to swallow, certainly motivating, past and present, many a recourse to religion, and its substitutes (like capitalistic consumerism, its current chief proxy[7]) and other chimeras, and the even greater absurdity of a caring god; but when the beater is a parent, or a representative of a parental authority, which role the modern republican nation-state has assumed, relaying such sheltering functions that once belonged to the aristocracy, then the shock is immeasurably amplified.

Here what enhances the horror of this primal scene of structural disillusionment is that the beating is being carried out officially and routinely, obviously as function of policy, but one, of course, that the beaters must have read between the lines, protecting the higher-ups from blame, as well as the useful democratic mask of a totalitarian system from an embarrassing transparency. Shrewdly the prisoners of this brig are always struck in the belly, where the blows are least likely to leave marks, but where the damage and humiliation are maximal—and as the prisoner gets the wind knocked out of him he can't talk either!

Whatever the ways any theatre, no matter how thoroughly faithful to the dogma of 'honesty', must dramatize reality in order to represent even a corner of it,[8] *The Brig* was a work, a performance and an 'event' that challenged its public, its critics and its creators (certainly its actors!) to look "behind the scenes", or, more exactly, *at* them, in a totally unprecedented way. First of all, this is a play that invites some serious reflection on what it means to be part of an audience for such a production. Obviously one doesn't just go to see *The Brig* for an evening out, for diversion or because it's the hottest ticket in town[9]—which would be tantamount practically to the effrontery of attending an electrocution for the fun of it, the way crowds used to be entertained at public hangings, beheadings, or by, in Roman times, a crucifixion. Of course, suffering, and sacrifice, certainly, is an old acquaintance of theatre's: etymologically the roots of Tragedy may lie in the sacrifice of a goat, later a human scapegoat. This is a tendency naturalistic theatre has only intensified, from the staging of the helpless pain in which the paralyzed mother of the adulterous pair who murdered her son watches the now married couple go about their daily business, in Zola's *Thérèse Raquin* (1873); to the syphilis-induced blindness that comes on the son at the end of Ibsen's *Ghosts* (1881); to the acting out of murder by poisoning and especially infanticide by smothering in Tolstoy's *Power of Darkness* (1887);

to little Miss Julie, commanded by her upstart lover to kill herself, who exits obediently into the dawn at the end of the play by Strindberg (1888); to the women who pass their lives waiting, in Synge's *Riders to the Sea* (1903-4), for the inevitable word that their men have drowned; to the moribund woman, denizen of Gorky's *Lower Depths* (1902), whose agony on stage, in public (her class not being able to afford the bourgeois comforts of privacy, even, or especially at such times) overshadows the first act of the play.

Nevertheless, in the whole history of theatre, including its "cruel" naturalist avatar, never has pain appeared with less apology or excuse, less redeemed by the aesthetic, religious, philosophical or even political[10] consolations of language and 'civilization' than in its raw depiction in *The Brig*, for which the only reason is that there is none, as for the (in)famous answer to Primo Levi's question (as to why he was not allowed to look out of a window) to a concentration camp guard: "In Auschwitz there is no *why*." An audience of such a play as *The Brig* is more there as *martyr*, in the ancient 'witness' sense of the word; ill-advised is anyone who has come just to enjoy the show; for this is a play that turns its back on its audience, like the performance of some kind of serious surgery, the quality of which, of course, would not be affected (we'd hope!) by the presence of an amphitheatre of medical students or other observers; it describes events that would have happened originally with no audience present, in fact could only have so transpired—for the first rule of oppression is to eliminate the chance of its being witnessed (unless, of course it's meant as an example), and a fortiori reported (a journalist's lot is often not a happy one). This overall concept of the irrelevancy of an audience, as if *de trop*, or beside the point, the way a witness to an accident is, especially if he can do nothing to help the situation, was already a significant factor in Wesker's plays, essentially about a day in the life of the British working classes, but there this aspect of the bystander audience was attenuated by many moments that would engage it more directly, which could have come straight out of the classical repertoire, even a Shakespearian one, as when, in *Chips With Everything*, the sincerity of Pip's commitment to "the common" man is savaged by an officer, who injures the protagonist's confidence in himself as cruelly as Iago attacked Othello's.[11]

Here, in *The Brig*, this process of audience effacement has evolved distinctly further, as if theatre, confessing finally its inability, because of structural limits it cannot but stay within, to realize its naturalist ideal of breaking down the distinction between play and audience, is dispensing with its audience altogether. Such a play has the quality, as for an accident, of something we might pass by and/or catch a glimpse of on our quotidian trajectories or something we might see riding by, or even from a window at home, or at our front doors, of people being harassed or arrested—maybe even being beaten gratuitously by the cops, or just another scene of random violence, more or less sudden sickness, misfortune or misery. Strokes differing for different folks, or for the same ones in different moods and ages, and at different times, some just pass on their way with nary a glance in the rearview mirror of their minds, others shed a more or less useless tear or two. Others, sadists or masochists of varying stripes, might gape for the entertainment or gratification value; a Schopenhauer find more evidence, as if any more were needed, for the fundamental unhappiness of the human condition. Your ethically model spectator might linger only so long as he or she thought they might be of some assistance in the situation, with the condition most 'sensible' people, not heroes, would make that it should be without undue or excessive risk to themselves; but always, categorically (in a Kantian sense), ignored or not, or an existential one (Camus-Sartre, certainly Levinas[12]), a perceived misfortune, injustice or other blatant misery and public suffering must call out to its beholder, implicitly or explicitly: "What are you going to do about me?"[13]. It seems to me that *this* is just about the most challenging aspect of a naturalist theatre that had been hammering away at the separations between drama and reality for almost a century before *The Brig* delivered its battering ram against those walls, and with all the nerve, revolutionary energy, courage and imagination of The Living Theatre behind that breakthrough blow: that is to pose *this* question, ever more insistently and adamantly, one that is increasingly difficult, if not impossible, for any audience-bystander to avert, ignore, or otherwise forget. This theatre becomes finally like our children whose problems we cannot ignore because we have had such a major role in raising them. It's we who maintain financially and certainly in very many other direct and indirect ways these brigs of all sorts.

This *situation*, predicament or quandary in which such a theatre puts its audience, turned into witnesses and/or bystanders, hardly innocent ones, since they are the taxpayers who support it, is greatly intensified when the historical and political context is, at least very conceivably, revolutionary: that is at a time and place when such powerful challenges have been mounted against prevailing oppressive systems that significant changes are in prospect, even might seem to be in process (or) turn out to be imminent.[14]

Such indeed had been the atmosphere and general political climate suffusing the conception, birth, staging and development of André Antoine's 'cradle' of the naturalistic Théâtre Libre, in France, with its watershed productions, for example of Tolstoy's *Power of Darkness* (1885) and especially the immensely insurrectionary *Weavers* (1892) of Hauptmann, where the demands made on its public are far from satisfied when the curtain has fallen and the audience has applauded the bowing or curtseying actors. A baby smothered on stage, or right under it, heard expiring, essentially because the world, as so constituted, has no room for it[15] in *Power of Darkness*; proletarians ready to attack the army and perish in the cause of freedom from oppression and exploitation, in *The Weavers*—these are the kinds of scenes and images that will surely follow the audience out into the street.

As will later become the constant Brechtian message, it is when the play is over that the real show begins; it can't be denied, accordingly, for example, that *The Weavers*, performed in politically conscious Paris halfway between the insurrectionary Commune and Civil War of 1870 and the Russian Revolution of 1917 was surely a dramatic reliving and reenactment of the ideals and ideas of the *Communist Manifesto*, of the revolutionary year of 1848; which manifesto was the "gold", refined in the alembic of proletarian revolt in the Silesian Weavers' Rebellion of a few years earlier, coincidentally become the very rich vein "struck" at the same moment by Marx and Engels that made their meeting in Paris[16] a true meeting of the minds—one whose awesome outcome was the realization whose ghost continues to haunt us today,[17] even after the "fall" of Communism, that the oppressed proletarians can, and therefore must, liberate themselves, without waiting to be led from above, as even the "Left Hegelians", attacked also by Marx in *The German Ideology*, thought indispensable.

A decade after the epoch of the Théâtre Libre, in another country and another theatre, The Moscow Art Theatre, but in a revolutionary climate that had changed from simmering to boiling, another masterpiece of naturalist drama, Gorky's *Lower Depths*, thrilled and galvanized its audience even more thoroughly. The author of the play, as no doubt some of its performers and producers, as well as certainly many in the audience that gave it such a thunderous ovation on its opening night in 1902, were headed for years in the Tsar's prisons, for exile and underground agitation and struggle in preparation for the Russian Revolution of 1917, expected then to be a prelude and a preparation for a worldwide one. This indeed was a theatre that was interchangeable with daily life, a life that could only be lived as political through and through; and *The Lower Depths*, absolutely, was a play that called out, in so many registers and ways, to its public to "do something about" what is indubitably presented as scenes and situations of socially generated misery and humiliation.

A third great peak in naturalist theatre, after the Théâtre Libre and the Moscow Arts Theatre, was The Living Theatre (USA),[18] of the 1960's and 70's.[19] These were, of course, as anyone who lived through them can confirm, profoundly revolutionary decades, and in so many ways— spearheaded, first of all, it seems to me, by massive distribution and consumption of psychedelic drugs that weaned the minds of millions away from blind obedience to the irrational commands of Capital, giving us a taste, albeit a fleeting one, of the "Paradise Now", the hallowed Communist dream of a classless society of love, peace and tolerance, whose motto would be "from each according to his ability, to each according to his need." There came the breakthroughs of the Civil Rights, Equal Rights, women and gay rights movements that were stirring things up and even marking some victories in the battles against racism, discrimination and sexism; followed by the mass anti-war manifestations, direct (Weathermen, draft resistors and draft-card burners) and indirect (tax noncompliance, 'dropping out' on drugs etc.) action and behavior, aimed as much at changing America as ending the Vietnam War.

The Living Theatre was of course in the very middle of all of this, prompting no doubt even a good bit of it, busted for nudity in Rio, New Haven and Philadelphia, centerstage even in the May '68, in France (Rostagno, *passim*), whence it had fled after the IRS siege of their performance space in New York City, in 1964, following the incitation and provocation of their signature productions of *The Brig* and, to cite an earlier and equally controversial production, *The Connection*, among others,. This play, by Jack Gelber, performed first in 1959, was a masterful kind of updating of Gorky's *Lower Depths* to a heroin and jazz scene, set in something like Greenwich Village of the late 50's. Strictly speaking, not naturalist, what with skilled, albeit "stoned" musicians sitting around a (heroin) "shooting gallery" of a pad, playing exquisite ensembles, when they're not improvising beautifully on their own instruments, it does blatantly cross into a "naked lunch" of a reality, with actors playing junkies so authentically they are sticking homemade (eyedropper—needle—rubber band jobs, yet[20]) syringes into their arms, and living in the kind of desperate present you would associate with the last days of a world. Naturalist also is the call as urgent as it was when it was coming out of *The Lower Depths* a half a century earlier for its public to do more than merely be diverted or consoled by such manifest hopelessness.[21]

With, however, *The Brig*, the naturalism, and with it the urgency of the call to the other, is at its purest, so pure and undiluted (with artifice) that it might even seem almost beyond naturalism, in the realm of some kind of formalist, cruel or expressionist theatre (and surely those associated with the production did not think of themselves in the tradition of Zola et al), the way an excess of virtue (the Puritan, Malvolio's, for example, in *Twelfth Night*) turns out to be a vice; here the excess is of reality, of a more real than the real, or hyper-real, as Baudrillard was to call this effect later—that is, of an illusion, uncanny and strange precisely through its familiarity and truthfulness, as of a copy overtaking its original. Here any distinction between audience and play has been erased, or rendered nugatory, simply because the audience of such a spectacle has entered into a kind of shadow or virtual reality whereby it has ceased to exist in any noticeable way, for this is a production that represents a reality that structurally is hermetically sealed from witness, that transpires in a dimension beyond the eyes of man (except those within it, who, by definition, either cannot talk or would never be heard if they did), like so much else that goes on in the underbelly of society. As well as being specific, existential, unreachable and untouchable, like a film about a catastrophe or disaster somewhere else, long ago, and on the verge of being unwatchable and un-listenable  (the truly disgusting beatings, the shouting etc.) what goes on in this brig is, as has become ever more obvious in the almost half-century since its first performance, infinitely generalizable. *The Brig* is now much more than just a metaphor or a symbol, which is maybe what once it was, for our inhuman and cruel societies of control and surveillance, now totally exploitative and oppressive of everyone's waking (if not sleeping) life.  It's become the very mirror in which we can all see ourselves, what has been done to us, or what we have allowed to be done— what's been our past and what the future has in store—more of the same, apparently, much more...  For what other message is this play putting out now than that we are all in the brig today, all in lock step, utterly programmed and conditioned, with our only hope, should we not rattle our chains too loudly, 'graduating' to what we've been sold as some kind of (bought and paid for) freedom but that is really just another section of our great prison of a world,[22] as in the more salubrious, higher circles of Dante's *Inferno* ("air conditioned nightmare", anyone?)?  Alternatively, there are always lower levels in hell for those who insist on remembering their names. There's the straightjacket, crazy house, then likely frontal lobotomy and/or electroshock treatment (popular 'therapies' of the 40's and 50's, currently being 're-evaluated' it might be interesting to know); now, total robotization courtesy of medication, media or both working in tandem.  We're thinking, of course, of, our pathetic Prisoner Six, who's committed the mortal and so unforgivable sin, of insisting he is someone after all, by calling out his name. If there has been a more meaningful, moving and political (in the highest humanist and liberating sense of the word) moment ever represented in the history of theatre, or of humanity period, we would like to know what it is: "My name is not Six. It's James Turner. Let me out of here...." (Brown :73) "James Turner," of course, is humored as such by a cunning guard, the way our cunning system allows us to play at being "ourselves" for a brief vacation, earned by keeping our shoulders to the wheel all year long, before being strapped on a stretcher and carted away—though one can't help wondering what would happen if all (we) prisoners were to attack the (necessarily) outnumbered guards together... We who have "nothing to lose but our chains" anyway!

# XI. "Like a Neutron Bomb of the Mind": A Digression on Stiegler

This liberating, but all-too-transitory moment we have just been celebrating in *The Brig* prophetically confirms the 'diagnosis' that the French philosopher, Bernard Stiegler, has been making, for a decade or so, in numerous writings (for instance, recently in *Aimer, Nous Aimer*), of the malaise of our times: in a word, that the destructiveness and self-destructiveness of humanity today rises out of a "wounded narcissism"[1] (*narcissisme blessé*), caused by a hyper-synchronization, resulting from our technology, one that tends to level anything special or particular about us: "a kind of neutron bomb of the mind, leaving after its explosion an uninhabited matter and corporeity, a sort of world of automatons." (*La Technique et le temps*, *3*, p. 119, my trans ) Reclaiming the difference of our individuality, as "James Turner" does here, for example, would constitute the only effective resistance, which Stiegler calls *the combat*, against this devastating entropy. It's then a measure of just how threatening such claims 'to be someone' are that the system then and there, and of course, no less so here and now (perhaps in more subtle, but even more efficient ways), quashes them and those who dare to make them as soon as they surface...

However Stiegler would certainly *not* go along with our wishful thinking about overpowering the guards: such a proletarian attack would smack, for him, at least in today's political and cultural climate, more of Nietzschen 'ressentiment' than Communist revolution,[2] for capitalist commercial, information, communication and conditioning structures, for Stiegler, have destroyed the Marxist two class (owners of the means of production and those who are obliged to sell their labor there) hierarchical paradigm. Instead Stiegler talks of a "generalized proletarianism." As a result of the evolution (really devolution or involution) of the combined and intertwined workings of capitalism, technology and globalization we are now more or less well rewarded, or 'paid-off' servants of a world system that no one really owns; we all would be today, in Malcolm X's terms rather "house niggers" than "field niggers", the former of course lamenting over the burning of their masters' (who have now become merely renters like the rest of us!) house, the latter rejoicing. Today, Stiegler would have it, as there are no more rulers and ruled, bosses and workers, owners and renters in our Brave New World of synchronized media, machines, robotization, and automatons, the prisoners attacking the guards would be attacking themselves (as a matter of fact, in The Living Theatre productions the guards and prisoners changed roles on different nights)[3]. What we need to do instead is to educate the guards... One fights back, for Stiegler, moreover not by Luddism, wrecking the machines that have ruined us, but by using the machinery of technology,[4] somehow, in such innovative ways as to express ourselves as unique, irreplaceable individuals.[5] The struggle that matters, today, for Stiegler, would be waged, then, ostensibly not by groups, and certainly not by classes (since there is only one), but by individuals, hopefully masses of us, but each of us in our own (Leibnizian) monad of a universe, maybe like that famous "society of porcupines" of Freud, where we associate for warmth and security, but keep our distance with the pointy quills.

The problem is that unless there are lots of 'us' who see things this way, we would be too few to matter; and too many of us "house niggers" consider ourselves the masters (what with our stock portfolios etc.)[6], and even assuming we're all in the same proletarian boat today, there is no question but that *even* for Stiegler, (too) many still think they're on high dry ground or on some kind of better ship, maybe even a luxury cruise; and, as a matter of fact, he admits finally the likely hopelessness of his (our) position, addressing his reader pessimistically, if not desperately, it seems to me, in an unusually frank (bewilderingly so, as when we receive a confidence we don't know quite what to do with or how to think of!) recent apostrophe, in a section called depressingly "*Crushing Majority, Tiny Minority*", of a recent book:

[The reader] should not forget that, insofar as he is still has the capacity and the desire to read a book like *De la misère symbolique* [this one], that he represents a very small minority, and one very likely, unless something really extraordinary happens, on its way to extinction. (159, my trans.)

Such flattery as this one cannot really enjoy! For it puts that small section of the "generalized proletariat", the single class or lack of class we all belong to today, who are not in a state of false consciousness (Lukacs) or denial (Freud) of their situation (Sartre), whether the obviously secularist Stiegler wants it that way or not, in the place of a kind of mystic 'remnant' holding onto the faith while the (or at least their own ) world is coming to an end. It is a test all the more frustrating, infinite and endless, since in this age of the Aftermath of the Death of God (Nietzsche) no afterlife or 'other world' can console us now...

Stiegler's position relates to an ongoing controversy over just how obsolete class struggle now is or is not. Derrida (with whom Stiegler had been closely associated, even co-authoring a book with him[7]) declaring also himself to be, in *Specters of Marx*, "suspicious of the simple opposition of *dominant* and *dominated*" (55) had called, as a matter of fact, for a "new international" (a subtitle of the book, even), which would include people from all over and from all walks of life, dispensing accordingly in its humanist universality with "the ultimate support that would be the identity and the self-identity of a social class" (*ibid*):

> The New International will effectively be 'barely public'....without coordination, without party, without country, without national community....,without co-citizenship, *without common belonging to a class*... (cited and emphasis, Tom Lewis 147, from his essay "The Politics of Hauntology in Derrida's *Specters of Marxg*" )

Given the stakes, elisions and fact that Derrida protested at length against what he called "Lewis' s hurried and somewhat global readings" (Derrida , "Marx and Sons" 239) I think it's worthwhile quoting in its entirety the paragraph being raided:

> The 'New International' is not only that which is seeking a new international law through these crimes [Derrida has been regretting the increase in human misery, the other side of the coin of recent progress in technology etc.]. It is a link of affinity, suffering, and hope, a still discreet, almost secret link, as it was around 1848, but more and more visible, we have more than one sign of it. It is an untimely link, without status, without title, without name, barely public even if it is not clandestine, without contract, 'out of joint',[8] without coordination, without party, without country, without national community (International before, across, and beyond any national determination), without co-citizenship, without common belonging to a class. The name of new International is given here to what calls to the friendship of an alliance without institution among those who, even if they no longer believe or never believed in the socialist-Marxist International, in the dictatorship of the proletariat, in the messiano-eschatological role of the universal union of the proletarians of all lands, continue to be inspired by at least one of the spirits of Marx or of Marxism (they now know that there is *more than one*) and in order to ally themselves, in a new, concrete, and real way, even if this alliance no longer takes the form of a party or of a workers' international, but rather of a kind of counter-conjuration, in the (theoretical and practical) critique of the state of international law, the concepts of State and nation, and so forth: in order to renew this critique and especially to radicalize it." (*Specters of Marx*, 85-86).

This "*more than one*" ("of the spirits of Marx...") refers to an important little essay by Blanchot, "Marx's Three Voices" quoted extensively, it seems entirely in *Specters* (29-34, but in pieces)—the three voices being essentially: 1. the polemical-hortatory (call to revolution, insurrection etc.); 2. the scholarly (history, economics...); 3. the prophetic (visions of the paradise of a classless society to come)—*voices*, however contradictory to each other they inevitably are sometimes, which should not be allowed to drown each other out.   The way he sees it, Derrida would not be so much negating the idea of proletarian, 'working class' politics and solidarity as listening to other voices, deploying other models, as (Blanchot points out) did Marx.

This 'revisionism' (if I may call it that, not necessarily pejoratively) of Derrida's has been more or less hotly contested, and certainly very much qualified, for instance, in *Ghostly Demarcations*, a collection of essays by a variety of Marxist authors.   Tom Lewis, for example, will speak there of a working class that needs to be defined differently now, because of the evolution of Capitalism, technology and the nature of today's 'globalized' labor market. For Lewis this contemporary working class would thereby be expanding rather than contracting or becoming obsolete —for instance, a working class should now include many if not most from minority or oppressed groups that are currently being heard from:

> Indeed, the overwhelming number of lesbians, bisexuals and gays, Native American, Latinos, Asians and Blacks, as well as women with jobs, belong to the working class. (Lewis 151)

Additionally the division is not so clear-cut today between mental and manual labor, so that the classic division of labor, roughly parallel to the dichotomy between those who own (or work closely and identify with— management) the means of production and those who are obliged to sell their labor there, would need to be revised; this expanding 'mental' role for what are still proletarians has amplified in some essential ways its power to attack Capital, and that exponentially; now, for instance a single technology worker, turned radical hacker might be able to damage a computer-based hegemony more effectively than a thousand workers of the past could threaten the ownership of the means of production!   Or even on the production line:

> Each individual blue collar worker who remains is now ten, twenty, or even a hundred times more powerful in terms of the ability to shut down production than each of the individual workers who were replaced by the machines operated by the remaining worker. (Lewis 151)

Well, *indeed*, the consequences of downplaying, bypassing, transcending or otherwise dumping such *red threads* and guiding concepts as class war and proletarian revolution have been for the better part of a few centuries now do seem to have been a lapse or fall into some kind fatalism or desperate mysticism of the self-elected remnant—with Stiegler's ambition, one which he just about admits is doomed, to 'fight' for change through acts in which individuals try to heal their wounded narcissism—as if the choice is between mysticism and revolution, excluding any third. On the other hand, let us beware of lapsing into an abstract humanist idealism, insufficiently anchored in the concrete struggles of the day and the working people who bear the brunt of them, and pay the lion's share of the price for them[9], to make much of a *difference* (to confront Derrida with his favorite word). Derrida's appeal for a 'classless' New Internationale, however intriguing and existentially 'upbuilding' (in the sense of Kierkegaard), doesn't it rather beg the question, in the tradition of an even more idealistic (though significantly, imaginary) forerunner, Don Quixote, that classes let go of power without it having to be wrested from them, and then guarded jealously by force of law, moral example, *and* arms? Remember the fate of the whipped farm worker our Knight of the Sad Countenance had freed, who was in for an even more savage beating once his liberator had ridden on... Anyway, unfortunately or not, it's as surely meaningful today as when Hegel enunciated that tragic law that we humans are so constituted that we cannot take anyone seriously, or be so taken ourselves, who does not put their life on the line for their beliefs.[10] This was indeed the very core of the Master-Slave Dialectic, which Marx was to stand later and for later generations so adroitly "on its head", courtesy of the Silesian Weavers' Revolt of 1844, thereby creating with his fellow weaver-enthusiast, Engels, the international Communist Revolution, whose principles of Class War were to be inscribed in that "Declaration of (Proletarian) Independence", *The Communist Manifesto*, of 1848. Following Hegel, who was following Aristotle, a master is a master because he is ready to give his life to remain one: "live free or die" must always be his motto. On the other hand, what makes a slave a slave is the choice of life, no matter how fettered and degraded, over death or risking it.[11] The Silesian Weavers had risked (and of course many paid with) their lives by attacking the masters (owners) of the means of production, and refusing to be "bought" off or otherwise co-opted or recuperated, had gone on to sack "their" warehouses and factories; furthermore, in a moment dramatized so effectively in Hauptmann's naturalistic masterpiece, *The Weavers*, they showed themselves fully ready to battle with the armies of Capital to protect their nascent revolution.

So alas, after all these millennia of progress, from the Pyramids to the Internet, we have still only our lives to give and to offer, and the price of freedom is still not gold, but blood.[12] Where, indeed, would Christianity be without Jesus and the martyrs; Islam without Ali and his massacred followers; the Labor movement without the "fusillés" of the Paris Commune and Sacco and Vanzetti; the Palestinian cause without its countless resistance fighters; or even Judaism today without the desperation of 17th century messianic Sabbatianism, which drew half of European Jewry, leaving everything, on the road to Jerusalem,[13] or, closer to "home", the Warsaw Ghetto uprising; African-Americans without Nat Turner and John Brown; or Civil Rights and racial equality without Martin Luther King, Medgar Evers, Rosa Parks and Malcolm X; philosophy (or even science) without Socrates, Giordano Bruno (burned at the stake, 1600) and Spinoza; the hopes of prisoners (of all sorts) everywhere to be free men and women, were it not for the "James Turners" who refuse to go on being merely numbers?

# XII. On the Side of the Object:
## *The Contractor, Changing Room*

With the theatre of David Storey, especially in watershed works of profound originality and innovation, like *The Contractor* (1969) and *The Changing Room* (1971), Zola's catalytic idea of breaking down the barriers between stage and reality reaches so perfect and total a realization that naturalism just about becomes a parody of itself[1], having evolved into a *style*, in the words of Stanley Kauffmann, "a new naturalism....[which] becomes perforce as sheerly aesthetic a mode as any that would have pleased Pater or Wilde"[2], ultimately one emptied of its traditionally radical content:

> The pleasure in watching *The Changing Room* was a pleasure in abstraction, not in reproduction; in stylistic exercise, not in any of the historical "scientific" aims of naturalism. And thus that pleasure, rather than being dusty with century-old courage, became ultra-contemporary and free: The creation of a para-world that merely resembles, more than is usual in the theater, the world outside, but whose purpose is to reward by *not* being the world outside, by being created by artists within its own perimeters....
>
> The New Naturalism, new because of the changed context, has long been an accepted mode in the contemporary graphic arts—in the sculpture of Kienholz and Segal, for example....Their painstaking, minute reproduction of reality becomes, by their act of reproduction, an abstraction from reality...[3]

While characters and the rudiments of a few story lines (that don't really go anywhere[4]) are still present in the plays, or are not entirely absent, what really happens and counts on this stage are activities. Here, things get done, first of all, where "ours is not to reason why"— *The Contractor*, for instance, requires that a tent, large enough for a wedding and reception to be conceived as going to take place within it, be erected on stage, achieving this in timely fashion and *in real time*, just as much of a *tour de force* of a performance as a dramatic event. Similarly in *The Changing Room* a rugby team changes, on stage, out of street clothes, then after the game (which happens between the acts) back into them.

The dynamics of whatever is happening on stage in such a theatre of photo or documentary realism has been turned topsy-turvy, a world truly "turned upside down". For here the background has become the foreground, the context the text, the environment, the institution and institutional goals seizing center stage, where the spotlight and focus is on everyone and no one. Dramatic tension, what there is of it, must be located in the stress between the team and its purpose, having to do with the kind of resistance more or less compliant matter is putting up to striving and contriving humanity that day, hour, minute, second; while, here, whatever happens between people is meaningful, and in the long run, interesting only in terms of results, of getting the job done. This kind of stage and staging, if not immoral, is certainly amoral: one would, I'd think have to look long and hard through these plays preeminently, but also into Storey's other dramatic creations, and also his prolific fiction for anything resembling right or wrong.[5]

Here all human rapports, relations, conflicts and stresses are secondary and subservient to a common project, a net with tight enough meshes that nobody falls through it. So it is that while Harry, the 'cleaner' in *The Changing Room*, who hands out towels and fresh uniforms etc., is described as being a total political paranoid, convinced, for instance, that the Russians are spraying the air with a special gas, so as to paralyze the West, no one questions his 'performance', probably all the more effective since the locker room is his whole world (he had never even watched a game). In *The Contractor*, Glendenning, said to be, in the stage directions, "a half wit" is alternatively mocked, coddled, derided and exploited by the boss and construction team alike. Such characters as these, of course, have been so indelibly marked by fate and/or genes that it's truly impossible to imagine leaving them any different from the way we found them; but even more normal types in these plays seem untouchable, except by their situation, which is their circumstances, in other words only to be affected externally— no epiphanies here, watershed moments, leaps in understanding or personal development. Thus tensions, in *The Changing Room*, maybe even incipient conflicts, are present in the changing (only their clothes) rugby team, for instance between young and old players, in the sense of competition for playing time, or between players, perhaps with family and maybe some education and more of a home or social life, and those who seem to belong totally to the "rugby life" because they have no other. While in *The Contractor*, strife breaks out openly, almost leading to violence, between a worker whose wife has recently left him and other workers who are teasing him mercilessly about it, or between the foreman, who has served time in prison, and his underlings, who want him to talk about his past. However, it's just as clear that the job, the game, the institution must constitute something like a contemporary equivalent of the Eastern "peace that passes understanding",[6] since all opposition and difference yields on this stage, and is subsided in favor of the common goal; while it is equally clear that once the project has been completed, even if nothing really has been resolved between people or by people, further association on the basis of another team effort seems both inevitable and necessary.

Not surprisingly, it's frequently been noticed, and sometimes complained, that nothing *happens* in David Storey's plays. They're all more rather than less "a day (or less) in the life", for instance, of rugby players and supporting staff, including even owner, who's just another way of looking at things (*The Changing Room*); workers putting up a tent, while the contractor and his family, including his wife, errant son, senile father, bride-to-be daughter and her not-too-promising fiancé wander on and off the stage-workplace, construction site—all of those places quite literally and figuratively (*The Contractor*); sons coming home for a parents anniversary, arguing among themselves and with their folks over the way they were raised and so forth (*In Celebration*); mental patients sustaining, at what cost!, as normal a conversation as they can manage (*Home*); even in *Cromwell* (1973), set in 17th century civil war England, very little happens, people mostly sit around and wait, keeping up the chatter, and we never meet the awesome title character. The closest thing to an event in his theatre must have been in his very first play, *The Restoration of Arnold Middleton* (1967), where perhaps the author did not yet have the courage of his dramatic convictions. In it the hero does exactly what the title indicates, coming back to his senses at the end of the play, maybe not very convincingly,[7] after a kind of middle-age crisis, one that was presented as conditioned and produced by the "sick society." Another glaring exception to this rule of nothing is *Life Class* (1975), where a nude model is 'raped' (she may have been in collusion with her attacker) on stage while the instructor and class look on without interfering, the former losing his job because of the incident. However the intention here was just as certainly parody, as Storey was clearly trying to give the critics who were complaining (more than!) what they were asking for.

However, there is no question that in the theatre that is most quintessentially Storey, especially with the works particularly under discussion here, *The Changing Room* and *The Contractor*, where the originality is maximal, unquestionable and unchallenged,[8] there is a kind of Brave New World surfacing, one where, as the French Situationists, with Guy Debord, were saying at about the time these plays were first staged, "nothing ever has happened or will happen". As slim as that possibility may be, by contrast, in *Waiting for Godot*, Godot might conceivably arrive, worth waiting for or not, certainly Lucky and Pozzo may well take a day off, distinguishing today from yesterday, before anything changes in *The Changing Room*, for here there will be always another game, if not always for the same, then for different players. Likewise for the workers putting up and pulling down the tent, for *The Contractor*, nothing marked that day as anything but another in an endless series, one with no end and which one can't imagine beginning, the way a horizon always recedes, out of reach, so you might as well give up imagining attaining it. There is nothing, indeed, to mark the day of these plays from any other day. The rugby players undress, nurse injuries, josh with each other more or less cruelly, suit up, one of them has his nose smashed (ending a career, which however was already waning, so a little bit of pathos here, maybe as close to dramatic as the play gets—but no *Requiem for a Heavyweight!*), they come back from the field, undress again, showering—certainly the fact that someone pees in the shower doesn't make the day memorable, then off to their private lives, as it's happened always and will always happen. Similarly, in *The Contractor*; absolutely nothing makes this day memorable. These workers, it is clearly said, have a hard time finding work (and/or work finding them), so it is not surprising that the foreman turns out to be an ex-con, that one of the workers is a half-wit, another's wife just left him, and a few others find an outlet for their hostility over being at the bottom of the social ladder by taking their aggressions out on others by "pressing on their buttons," or prying into their secrets. Such a world is presented as uncreated, unchangeable, one that can only be adjusted to, but not really defied or challenged, as if one were to wake up in a game that was already in progress, or at a work site in operation.

Freedom, originality, individual initiative and originality—in other words, all those hallowed humanist entities—are a thing of the past, or are rather as if they never existed. Here, there is no "lighting up one's cigar" (no smoking today anyway, under the Tyranny of Health), as in Brecht's metaphor for the *verfremdungseffekt*, whereby events can be contemplated from a distance sufficient enough for the audience to become aware of the conditional nature of all "reality" and therefore the possibility, even desirability of altering it. Reality in such a world has assumed the (invisible) mantle of the Absolute, as unquestionable and as silly to contest or challenge as the traffic light on the corner: "you don't want to get run over, do you?", such a reality says to jaywalking rebels, or at least cross at the corner with the light and between the lines so you can sue whoever hits you. This again, once more again, yet again, is the world of 'nothing special', 'no big deal', and the way it's always been and will always be, the world of 'go fight city hall'.

That this represents a distinct evolution beyond theatre of Arnold Wesker should come as no surprise, since Wesker's plays, however 'ordinary' and quotidian, in the sense of "kitchen-sink realism", retain much of what has traditionally made theatre theatre, comedy comedy, and tragedy tragedy; his environments, social and historical contexts are always significant, but only to the point that they give his protagonists something to struggle against and win or (usually) lose. Here things happen, and irreversibly: the revolution has failed and TV culture has taken over, by the end of the *Chicken Soup*

*With Barley*, the army has won out over the individual who has rebelled against its class structure after *Chips with Everything*, and Ronnie's farewell to the proletarian woman he has seduced before and abandoned by the end of *Roots*, is definitive; while the cook Peter has been the Samson bringing the kitchen Temple of Capitalism down on Philistines in *The Kitchen*, where there is no chance of his ever working again!

The ten telling years of the sixties separate the anarchist revolution of Wesker's *Kitchen* (1959) from the end of ideology of Storey's *Contractor* (1969). Perhaps we can call this the naïveté gap, or the disillusionment, or cynicism gap of some dawning, maybe long overdue 'age of suspicion'. The fact plainly is that between the naturalism of Wesker and that of Storey there has been some kind of sea-change; in the former people are still in a dialectical relation with institutions, objects and things, with which they bargain, struggle, negotiate and coexist in an endless cycle of victories and defeats that are never definitive; in the latter, to invoke the convenient language of Baudrillard[9] once more, the subject seems to have collapsed totally, or fallen back on the object, so that things, institutions, codes, settings are all there is. Better get used to it, bud!

Closer to this abstract mood of Storey's style and stylization, philosophically and politically, would be the universe of Kenneth Brown's *Brig*. With Storey and Brown, we come to the watershed moment in our (non-comprehensive[10]) survey of naturalist drama—of a break from the humanist and the human and a drift to the side of the object. For as in the plays of Storey, surely most characteristically what dominates in *The Brig* is (prophetically, ahead of its time, as per *Brave New World* and *1984*) the context, the institution, the mechanism and machine. The single pathetic voice of rebellion, crying in the wilderness, that we have tried to make so much of, for lack of any other straws to clutch at, this James Turner who dares to say his name, is reduced, and rapidly, as far as that play is concerned to being a mere malfunction in an otherwise smooth running system, perhaps like the cry of a doll, which, pressed in the right place, will disturb the program of the other puppets and automatons, if only momentarily. Such imperfections, become 'learning experiences' are inevitable glitches in the functioning of any system on its way to total control of the human animal, in other words elimination of what is human about him, his serendipity and unpredictability. However the theatre of *The Brig* will still seem a *living* one compared to the pacified, aesthetic, poetic, symbolic naturalism of Storey,[11] overwhelming and determining by reason of its very routine matter-of-factness. A jail we can rebel against, in fact we're supposed to rebel against, which is why they build them with such high walls and in such remote places; in fact certain types of prisoners (of war) are allowed to (try to) escape, and might even be disgraced if they don't (at least try). Similarly, we can rebel against the very oppressive, not to mention sexist environment of the *kitchen*[12] of a large restaurant, against the hypocrisy of bourgeois sexual repression (*Thérèse Raquin, Ghosts, Miss Julie, Mrs. Warren's Profession*), against an oppressive society that puts its outcasts to death early and frequently (*Riders to the Sea*), while depriving them of all privacy and dignity, even in dying (*The Lower Depths*), or despoils its workers (*The Weavers*) or even a 'liberal' one that extends to the rich the same right to sleep under a bridge as a pauper, or allows the fascists to demonstrate against Jews in the Jewish East End of London (*Chicken Soup With Barley*)—one can rebel. But how to protest against a *changing room*, against *a tent* going up, against three sons returning home *in celebration* of their parents' wedding anniversary, or against a few mentally deranged people trying to keep a little conversation going and not to cry too much in the garden of a mental hospital, their only *home* left in a hostile world?

Peculiarly, but suitably when you think about it, objects *do* dominate in the theatre of Storey, and from the very beginning, with a weird set of medieval armor that is the strange centerpiece of the *Restoration of Arnold Middleton*, which Arnold keeps promising his wife to get rid of, and never can quite bring himself to. Then there's the 'weightlifter' madman Alfred, dottier clearly than the other loonies, because incapable of carrying on even the pretense of a conversation, who compulsively lifts the garden furniture in *Home*, while the others gape on silently; significantly, when he removes the furniture, the show is over:

ALFRED
    Take them back.
*(He indicates their two wicker chairs.)*
HARRY
    Oh, yes...
ALFRED
    Don't take them back; get into trouble.
JACK
    Oh, my word. (ALFRED, *watching them, lifts the metal chair with one hand, holding its legs, and demonstrates his strength. They watch in silence.* ALFRED *lifts the chair above his head; then, still watching them he turns and goes.)*
Shadows[13]

It's these objects that dominate and in the end are memorable, not the people; for isn't it rather the *tent* that stays in our minds after *The Contractor*, the feat, technique and 'art' of putting it up, actually much more unique and special than any of the characters, who are all, as interesting as they are or are not, rooted in some kind of deeply familiar and traditional type. In *The Changing Room*, it's the massage tables, the bandages, showers, towels, the room itself which provides the novelty our memories will hold onto. The people, by contrast, turn out to be predictably familiar, like us and everyone else, exactly what their world has made of them, perhaps allowing some the illusion, at some point in their lives, usually early on, that they were freely choosing their fates...

Just as the subject in Storey has fallen into, or merged with, the object and/or institution or activity, so have the social classes fused, becoming indistinctly common allies in the eternal struggle against recalcitrant matter. However much solidarity there is or isn't among the workers, where, indeed, competition, backbiting and acrimony seem to prevail, whether in the changing room, tent-construction cite, family home (in *In Celebration* there is competition for the scarce respect/love of the parents), or mental asylum (in *Home*, especially the women slandering each other as 'sluts' to the 'eligible' male inmates), there seems to be harmony between the ruling class and the ruled, to whom they bring peace and harmony. Chairman Thornton, club owner, and Mackendrick, club secretary, are quite at home in the changing room, bantering, reassuring, healing, buddying and calming, very much unlike the players, always at each others throats; while Ewbank, ex-worker who has risen in the world, but who has not forgotten his roots, is quite clearly as at home on the construction site as any day laborer, as is his senile former rope-maker (that's how the family got into tents) father, who wanders around holding a good piece of rope, "like they don't make any more"; the whole family, wife, daughter, fiancé, errant (hippie-nonconformist) son are equally at home chatting with, relating to, the laborers, who get along better with the boss and his family than each other; the workers express opinions about the prospects of the marriage being a happy one, give the boss advice, or sympathy about the errant son etc., while tearing into each other at every opportunity, even cruelly mocking their half-wit comrade, whom as a matter of fact the family of the boss is kind to. There is clearly no more class war here, whatever there was has retreated to the war within the one working class,[14] a war that only the tranquilizing presence of its 'betters' keeps from turning into an open one, just as the presence of the boss in *The Contractor* was all that kept the foreman ex-con from firing a worker whose rude curiosity was getting on his nerves!

Nor does Storey make it possible for us to be fooled for even a minute by such occasional posturing as adopts the vocabulary of class war, disavowed by its very speakers when it's barely out of their mouths, for instance when the workmen are admiring the house of their employer:

BENNET
    A house like that, and you don't need to do any work...
MARSHALL
    Built up from what...?
FITZPATRICK
    (*gestures*).
    The windows bright with our sweat
    The concrete moistened by our sorrows.
MARSHALL
    Did you get that out of the papers?
FITZPATRICK
    I did.[15]

Such radical ideas as this one indeed gets "out of the papers" to let off
some inebriated steam for a minute or two.  No one is planning, however, to
throw rocks through the windows of the rich!  Today's "working class is the
bourgeoisie bereft of its possessions", Storey has said to an interviewer;[16]
and, in another play, *The Farm* (1974) there is an absolutely scathing
denunciation of a proletariat by a sympathetic character (Brenda), who very
obviously represents the scorn of its author:

> ...they couldn't be more accommodating if they'd been manufactured in that bloody
> factory.  They even go on strike like a flock of bloody sheep.  Strike—strike—
> strike—to show they're as mean-minded as everybody else: small, mean, bigoted,
> cheap materialistic.  When they've got something to strike about, like now
> [firings]—nothing.  Not a whimper." [p. 15]

In Storey's plays such struggle as takes place does so within classes,
rather than between them.  So, for example, between Bennet and Fitzpatrick,
workmen in *The Contractor*, there's a running battle of insult and injury
based on the domestic problems of the former and the resentments of the
latter; likewise, in *The Changing Room* there's an ongoing and evident
antagonism between the more and less cultured players on the rugby team.
Overall what rules here is a concept, or at least a commonly shared fantasy
that it is inconceivable not to accept, because no alternative to it exists, of a
single-class society.

Just as Storey's plays break down the separations between ruling and
working classes,[17] then subject and object, especially when that *object* is
*place*[18], they operate ultimately and perfectly, just about to the point where
they must verge on, or cross over into parody,[19] as a realization of the
naturalist ideal, announced initially by Zola, of effacing the distinctions
between stage and audience, theatre and actuality.

***

By now, of course, theatre is far from being the only place where
distinctions between representation and reality have been challenged, if not
totally effaced.  Film also has been pushing theatre to the sidelines on the
grounds of rendered reality[20] in the century or so since it became pandemic;
and seemingly, today, there is nothing it won't or can't represent or leave to
the imagination.  However, what theatre retained uniquely was the live
presence of the actors and the audience; the latter remaining, of course, to see
the film, yet it feels different to clap (or hoot) the actors taking their bows or
making their escape than a flat screen, not to mention for the actors
performing before a live audience, of whatever dimension (even one
composed of themselves/each other, eschewing the audience entirely, in

favor of 'inner search and development', as in late Grotowski), or a shouting director and a lot of machines and technicians. With the advent of TV, and then the interactive forms, like internet, snapshot taking, video-taping cell phones, which report and record the location of their operators as surely as whatever they are aimed at, whatnot, even this 'live', or at least 'present moment' quality of theatre has been challenged, unless you want to talk about retaking some of this ground (or yielding it) through the impact of the newer media upon the older and vice-versa.

For it would seem to follow from the citation from Baudrillard with which we opened this study (Chapter I), whose gist was, "Art has disappeared because Art is everywhere", that "Theatre is dead because Theatre is everywhere", in this Society of the Spectacle. We have become the players and the audience, everywhere reported, taped, photographed, conditioned, scripted and plotted—our comings and goings, increasingly electronically traceable, our phone calls, cash transactions, our very tumescence and detumescence a matter for the public to know about and applaud or not.[21]

Exploded, on the other hand, is the notion and illusion, one which the "political" naturalism of theatre did much to dispel also—with the grim reality of many of its depictions, that we, as audience, by the mere fact that we are afforded the right and privilege of being one, are protected from the catastrophe of a world that we have made and which has made us. A classic pleasure of tragic theatre, apart from the perversions of *schadenfreude* or the cleansings of *catharsis*, must have been the feeling that as the audience we are spared those sufferings; they are happening on the stage (but not really), so that they won't or can't happen to us, kind of like an apotropaically virtual sacrifice, or even the scapegoat or martyr of the Christian passion play. Reading the newspaper or, a fortiori *watching* the news afforded, then, that same comforting illusion of protection.[22] Here our insulation was even more comforting and reassuring, even thrilling, because seeing being believing, such dreadful things are happening in reality out there, but not to us, like watching a storm (or a battle) from a safe distance. However, the armor of this insulation turned out not to be equal to the challenge of the Total War upon populations of modern times; and so to the attacks of 9/11, where the images of bodies falling, then the spreading smoke and fire of the collapsing twin towers turned the "only watching" TV viewers into fleeing (when they were lucky) fugitives. The spectator becomes the spectacle,[23] or as the Rolling Stones sung so prophetically, it seems like ages ago: "Gimme Shelter"!

Before we plunge any deeper into Hegel's night in which all cows are black let's pause to consider, however, that if everything is art today then nothing is art, if everything is theatre then nothing is theatre. Clearly art continues, if not in the commercially vitiated form, so justly denounced by Baudrillard as being indistinguishable from business,[24] then as activity, protest and expression of certain threatened (by starvation, of diverse sorts) and menacing (challenging) elements; similarly theatre endures, if no longer as a major conduit and arena for our culture's most tormenting conflicts and most conflicting voices, as once in the Greece of *Agamemnon* and *Antigone*, the England of *Richard II* and *Hamlet*, or more recently, as we have seen from our front-row seat, in the high political stakes involved in naturalist plays by such as Hauptmann and Gorky of a century or so ago, then in significant currents and undercurrents, in which playwrights, directors, actors and producers, "theatre people", of all kinds, in short, are still paddling and swimming, underwater if need be, and upstream, resisting being swept to the seas of modern technology-driven estrangement and sinking there...

For theatre is still and will always be (until we evolve into a tongue-less, voice box-less species) a precious and irreplaceable reservoir for the spoken word[25], even or especially in its denial and/or silencing; as Blanchot would often insist, reminding us of its perdurability: 'eternity' (as far as we are concerned) and existence. So, finally, the competitive technologies and new media do not so much abolish theatre as force it to redefine itself, to decide what exactly is still unique about it that needs to be intensified and developed—the way photography enabled painting, once, freed from the task of representation, to become at once more abstract and more concrete. A naturalist theatre, a fortiori, would be even more challenged than others, whether classical or modern (symbolist, absurd, 'epic-Brechtian', ontological-hysteric, of cruelty etc.) by the reality show of contemporary technology; since naturalism purporting to represent a reality, ultimately, that is indistinguishable from the stage, it can more readily be "upstaged" by the newer media and inventions that don't even stop to represent reality, but instead transmit it directly, and in *actual* time.

However, naturalism in theatre was always already an aporia and a contradiction-in-terms, maybe like one of those P.I.C., or Principles of Insufficient Cause, to which Robert Musil wryly attributes such efficiency in getting things working, in *The Man Without Qualities*.[26] For *theatre*, related etymologically to the word *theory*, means, in fact, a place apart from everyday life and quotidian concerns,[27] whereas *naturalism* in theatre suggests that stage and reality are in one and the same place. In fact and in practice what this naturalism suggests is rather an ideal toward which this theatre should extend and tend, here verging on the philosophy of "as if", as expounded by Hans Vaihinger and Jules de Gaultier.[28]   Closer to our subject, is the 'epic theatre' framework of Brecht, especially as reworked by such imaginative innovators as Richard Foreman—according to whom the play should represent not exactly what is, but what should be... Turning this around, of course, naturalistic theatre touches on an inverted 'epic' by showing, with *The Brig* of Kenneth Brown and Gorky's *Lower Depths* rather what *should not be*...or should not be allowed to continue to be.

The very concept, for instance, of shaking up traditional separations between stage and audience, play and reality that we have so often returned to in these pages,[29] must occur in a theatre, or place apart; for in the world in which we all live and most or mostly try to survive, such separations are endemic and ineluctable. A derealizing theatrical practice can play with, float, take more or less seriously these separations; it can even *virtualize* stage and/or audience, imagining, as in experiments by Pirandello and others, the audience as actors, or sometimes dispense with an audience altogether[30]— not to mention script, writer and director entirely[31] —or, as in plays like *The Brig* of Brown and *The Changing Room* of Storey, where the stage virtually *turns its back* on the audience altogether, constituting, as it were a hermetically sealed universe, where the actors carry on like workers in a factory who are told not pay any attention to passerby or tourists who just want to see "how the thing is made."

Ultimately Naturalistic Theatre, a bit like Reality TV, is a contradiction in terms, an oxymoron. Like the "square circle" saying the words doesn't make them so, since theatre, together with what it calls the reality it's trying to represent (or transform, at the very least interpret), the audience it constitutes and treats more or less intimately or even denies totally, is in itself a place apart. Naturalist, or not, it is impossible to abolish, since you can't abolish something that didn't exist in the first place, except as a place apart; as long as you have a place you must have a place apart, since that's what a place is.

That place it's apart from, that it's still a part of, yes, *that*, wisdom of our time, can be abolished, and, unfortunately or not, it's not unreasonable to opine this is what is happening as I write and you peruse. The place we're all in, more or less long before vanishing can become altered, corrupted, polluted, fascist, sexist; or, more hopefully, if less likely, improved— becoming more welcoming, egalitarian, democratic and humane—but as long as there's a place for us to be, whether it seems to be in its last days, or in the first of many happy ones, by definition there must always be a place apart. For a place and a place apart, like clouds and rain (or sunshine) come and go together, like practice and theory, world and theatre. [32]

# Appendix

## 1. Rewriting Naturalism:Zola's *L'Assomoir* and Reade's *Drink*

*L'Assommoir*, by Émile Zola, tells the story of the life and death of a Parisian laundress over a period of about 20 years during the Second Empire. In his Preface of 1877 Zola states his goal as that of describing the "fateful downfall of a working family." The action of the novel is not so much plotted as it is presented as being a mere succession of random events without much sense or direction. Gervaise, the laundress, has been taken to Paris by her lover Lantier, where he abandons her, together with her two illegitimate children. She subsequently marries a roofer named Coupeau, who after an accidental fall, becomes a heavy drinker. At the same time she carries on a platonic affair with a blacksmith named Goujet, who all through the novel is there when she needs him the most and makes very few demands upon her. She has a third child, this one legitimate, by Coupeau—a girl named Nana, who by the time she is fifteen has turned into a prostitute. A noteworthy aspect of the novel is the menage à trois that Gervaise carries on with Coupeau and Lantier—when the latter suddenly comes back into her life. Gervaise has been set up in the laundry business by her "best friend" Goujet, and though things seem to go well for a while, the business slowly falls into bankruptcy, due to the tendency of the owners to consume their profits in pleasures. Lantier, for instance, reappears at the end of a magnificently described orgy of eating and drinking in celebration of Gervaise's birthday.

After the shop folds Gervaise and Coupeau move to a sixth floor apartment nearby, where among the residents there is an eight year old girl, Lalie Bijard, who is taking care of a two younger brothers and her entire household, due to the fact that her heavy drinking father has beaten her mother to death and the Lorilleux family, relatives of Coupeau and stingy gold-spinners, who examine scrupulously the soles of the shoes of visitors to their apartment for stray flakes of gold, and who embody the principles of free enterprise to an extreme never would even give a crust of bread to a starving man because it might interfere with his spirit of initiative. This is truly that world of "freedom" described by Anatole France as allowing the rich man to sleep under the same bridge or on the same park bench as a pauper...

Turning from this novel to Charles Reade's dramatic adaptation in English, *Drink* (1880), is instructive: there is a complete change both of manner and message. Whereas Zola presents us with a world in which the individual is seen as having no control over the elements which determine his or her existence—that is, an individual's behavior is seen as an outcome of the combination of forces working on him due to the influence of heredity and the place of his insertion into the environment and economy—Reade presents us with characters who are seemingly free to choose the lives they lead and merit praise or blame accordingly. Zola's masterfully drawn Goujet, for instance, the passive and basically helpless witness of his beloved Gervaise's slow disintegration becomes Reade's disgusting sentimental and moralistic preacher of temperance and will power. Goujet the worker has become in Reade's hands a sanctimonious capitalist who lectures the workers about virtue. In other ways also Zola's message is defused and denatured. Coupeau doesn't drift into drink, as he does in the novel through the working of the overwhelming influences upon him, but instead he is the victim of a plot to get him "hooked on the bottle." Reade has Gervaise as Lantier's wife, not mistress—and even goes so far as to invent a previous wife for Lantier so as to avoid the situation of bigamy when she marries Coupeau.

Reade also suppresses the menage à trois which is so central to the novel. Whereas Zola presents Gervaise as being a victim of her own and others' sexual urges and animal instincts—not to mention her profound death-wish that seems to lurk in the background and that finds expression in her gluttony and self-abasing promiscuity—Reade will put her on a pedestal of virtue and temperance. He simply doesn't deal with those darker aspects of the human psyche that so preoccupy Zola.

Likewise that quintessential victim of society, the eight year old head of the household Lolie Bijard, whose mother has been beaten to death by her father, and who is beaten to death in her turn, becomes in the play a teenage nightclub singer, Phoebe Sage, who by dint of hard work and perseverance, is managing to support her family. Gervaise herself in that pathetic penultimate chapter of the novel in which she unsuccessfully tries to sell a body which no one wants is changed in the play to a beggar who has fallen on some hard times. Finally, the theme of Nana's viciousness and early turn to prostitution is completely suppressed

The mutation of the powerful convincing beings of Zola into the dubious figments of Reade's wishful thinking is paralleled in the language they speak. The high-blown pseudo-poetic and romantic diction of the play, with a marked tendency to trite iambic rhythms and sentimental repetition is in marked contrast to the natural slang used by the characters in the novel. This is understandable in that Reade is still hanging on to an idealistic vision of humanity that Zola will have no part of. Though the novel is essentially plotless, we find in the play that Reade resorts to the theme of Virginie's revenge for being beaten up by Gervaise (Virginie, who worked as a laundress alongside of Gervaise as the novel opens, on the day of Lantier's abandonment of her, had taunted her with the revelation that she had also had sex with him) to explain almost all of the subsequent events. Thus Copeau's fall from the roof, which is presented by Zola as simply another link in the chain of unavoidable misfortunes, is presented by Reade as having been due to an intentional oversight on Virginie's part, who neglects to inform him about some weak scaffolding. Instead of killing himself with drink as he does in the novel, Reade has him murdered, with premeditation, by Virginie, who has replaced the relatively innocuous wine with the powerful brandy she gives to him as a "present."

Another marked contrast is observable with regard to Lantier. Whereas the novel closes with him being about the embark on his third menage à trois, that is after having devoured two marriages and two businesses he's in good appetite for a third portion of each, and is about to take up with a lady who is going to sell tripe (!) in the very same shop where Gervaise did laundry and Virginie sold candy—the play on the other hand has him being stabbed by Virginie's jealous husband, subsequent to Phoebe Sage's successful counterplot. Zola's typical victims of society, functionally incapable of fighting back, who can never win, only at best be temporarily lucky—these "doomed" men and women become in Reade's treatment characters of will and determination, those who are capable in the end of punishing the guilty and rewarding the innocent. All of this is meant to prove Goujet's line which ends the play and which Zola would never have subscribed to: "There is a providence—severe—but just"; but unfortunately, to adapt some sharp words of Sartre to this 'situation': God is not enough of a playwright to convince us of this; and neither is Charles Reade.[1]

## 2. Awakenings: *En Famille, La Casserole, Little Bugger* (Méténier)

The one-acts Oscar Méténier wrote for the Théâtre-Libre, *En Famille* (1887) and *La Casserole* (1888) were very much in the spirit of this naturalistic attack on the separations between stage and reality. The earlier play, about the guillotine, spared no details nor feelings in its matter-of-fact description of the execution of a "friend of the family". The later play, about the Parisian underworld[2] ("casserole" meaning informer), anticipating Cinéma Vérité, used non-actors, also modeling its sets and the behavior of the people in it after an actual location, a well-known wine bar, which was "researched," à la Zola:

> To play the bouncer, la Terreur de la Maube, Antoine brought in Leo Will, an underworld friend of Méténier's from his police days,[3] and one of the strongest men in Paris, or provided the shock of 'the thing itself' intruding on the imitation of the thing with a show-stopping sequence of weight-lifting that astonished the on- and off-stage audience alike.
>
> Antoine took the Chateau Rouge bar in the Maubert as the model for his set and sent Pinsard [who played the patron] to study the gestures and walk of Père Trolier, patron of the Chateau Rouge. The particularity of the bar was registered in the big double door leading to a dance-hall at the back of the stage....Within in, the characters smoked, drank and played cards, moved to and from the bar, the dance-hall or the street. [Chothia, p. 89]

In a series of little anarchist skits Méténier wrote late in the 1890's we can see even more clearly how the stage has melted into the surrounding environment, in refusing to indulge or tolerate any illusion of escape from it. When the characters speak, as we've noted above about *The Weavers*, it's not with their own voices, which they don't have, can't afford etc., but as representatives of their class. Ever a danger for these characters is false consciousness, especially when your girlfriend has just been delivered of a child, as in *Little Bugger*, where the character realizes that he has been thinking like a capitalist, in wishing to marry, so that he can name his son after himself, when his class position should have led him the other way— that is, to think like an anarchist, and not care about such "rich people's nonsense"!

# Notes

## Introduction: Ushering in the Spectacle

1   Anyone who thinks we're throwing this word around needs to peruse Lehmann's prime example of *hypernaturalism*, Werner Schwab—whose *Holy Mothers* (1990) features prominently a woman (Mariedl) whose specialty is unblocking toilets with her bare hands (proudly eschewing rubber gloves), the performer of a kind of hunger-artist of an invented spectator sport, described in lavishly detailed naturalistic gory glory; a brief 'sample": "So there's a huge crowd already waiting at the third toilet, and they shout their loudest when strong Mariedl puts her whole arm down the toilet, right to the armpit hairs." (28, but *passim* in play, Mariedl talking about practically nothing else, and liking to celebrate her achievements in 3$^{rd}$ person!). *Hypernaturalist* would I think describe much that is happening in theatre even more recently; for instance in the plays of Sarah Kane, or of Thomas Bradshaw, who has been called "a Sarah Kane with a sense of humor" for instance, *Southern Promises* (produced 2008, New York), centered on interracial relationships in the ante-bellum South, and even more extravagantly in *Prophet* (2005, New York), a play about a henpecked white man, whose wife does him the favor of dying in an accident (it turns out to be a practical joke, after he takes a seemingly more submissive Black mistress, but he winds up strangling her in her coffin when she 'wakes up' during the funeral). His God booms instructions at him from offstage to be the leader of a counter-revolutionary male supremacist movement, re-enslaving especially Black women, demonstrating his 'faith' by, like Abraham with Isaac, being willing to sacrifice his offspring, a beloved daughter; only this time God *allows* the sacrifice to be made! If Lehmann's quality of 'grotesque excess' be thought of as endemic to hypernaturalism, then no aspect in Bradshaw is more hypernaturalist than his depiction of sexuality, for instance in the latter play, the opening encounter between the protagonist, Alex, and his new Black girlfriend, Shanaqua, who he has just 'rescued' from ghetto life and oppression by a 'gangsta' Black boyfriend:

    *"(things are really getting heated between them. She is stroking his penis through his pants.)....*
ALEX
    I'm gonna fuck you in the ass so hard that you're gonna bleed.
SHANAQUA
    Yeah, keep talkin dirty to me. I love it.
ALEX

I will. After you put on your new clothes.
SHANIQUA
I don't know if I can wait. I need you to fuck me right now. Feel my wetness.
*(She sticks his hand down her pants and pulls it out after he feels her wetness. He then licks his finger.)*
ALEX
You taste like rosewater.
*(He gets up and comes back with tattered slave clothing and shackles.).* " [Scene 4]

2    *Leçons VII: le désir politique du Dieu* (1988): "...l'étroite parenté de termes d'origine grecque tels que *théorie* et *théâtre*" (p.235); my trans.

3    not its philosophical one, with a pedigree going back as least a far as Aristotle...but certainly not unconnected to its eventual and ongoing literary avatar.

4    When 'James Turner', a prisoner, against regulations, refuses to announce himself as a number, identifying himself by name, then is carted away, tied to a stretcher and fighting and screaming all the way, by MP's to the loony bin, crazy or not...as an obvious example to the other inmates (the rest of us! I'd say).

5    Both have been revived recently; *The Connection*, to mark the 50th anniversary of The Living Theatre (Feb. 2009).

6    "Whatever their motives, the Naturalists did choose poverty, deprivation and squalor for their subject matter far more than any of their predecessors." (Fürst and Skrine, *Naturalism*, p. 50).

7    Abirached, *op. cit.*, p. 253 ; my trans.

8    *Consuming Life* (2007); *Wasted Lives: Modernity and Its Outcasts* (2004)

9    I am paraphrasing his most recent book, *Multitude, Between Innovation and Negation* (2008) here; in his earlier (and very widely read) *Grammar of the Multitude* (2004, but based on a series of yet earlier lectures) he leaves room also for a certain kind, at least, of civil disobedience: "I am proposing two key-terms: civil disobedience and exit" (p. 69); however, the former he makes immediately clear is no issue-oriented action, in the style of Thoreau, Gandhi, M.L. King,; but, *not protesting anything in particular*, a systematic refusal to participate in the structures of control, something like a throwback to the rejection of 'the total wrong' Marx early on (a cause the French May '68, and Debord and the Situationists very much revived) thought of as being suffered by the worker under capitalism, one that cannot be redressed by improvements or reform.  See also Michael Hardt & Antonio Negri (a colleague and Italian Autonomist 'co-conspirator', who 'came up' with Virno ), *Empire* (2000) for these 'passive' strategies of desertion and exodus (p. 212); but for an articulate counterargument against them see Laclau, "Can Immanence Explain Social Struggles?" (27ff), in an anthology of frequently very critical answering texts to *Empire, Empire's New Clothes* (2004).   Another interesting essay in this collection, from the point of view of this 'exodus' strategy (certainly a better one for dealing with 'justice" and /or a parole board, as Negri, re-imprisoned in Italy by the time *Empire* came out, after returning there after long years as a fugitive in France, needed to...) of the Italian radical autonomists and their allies is Kam Shapiro's "The Myth of the Multitude", where the focus is on George Sorel, too much neglected in favor of more obvious inspirations like Deleuze-Guattari and Foucault, as a forerunner of Hardt and Negri's *Empire*; for Sorel, for example, proletarian (the "multitude" of today, "when we have all become proletarians", although Sorel did not include intellectuals, like himself as such) violence is what he calls a myth (The General Strike), which may be more or less effective strategically and politically; however he saw it as a *necessary* one in terms of a distancing and weaning away of the proletarians from a bourgeois ideology of compromise and reformism.  Like Grotowski's theatre, which wound up being about changing the actor, Sorel's violence is first and foremost about raising the consciousness of the political actors of our time, and keeping it at peak levels—the proletarians: "Proletarian violence confines employers to their role as producers, and tends to restore

the separation of the classes, just when they seemed on the point of intermingling in the democratic marsh. " (Shapiro 303, citing Sorel, *Reflections on Violence* [1908])

10  Theatres have always been dangerous places, which is why they were once shut during times of plague; and fire departments are so nervous about them; but *a fortiori* so when the world becomes theatre!

11  and don't we make art out of that too! witness the recent exhibition of photographs of these 'exits': "Falling Bodies"...

12  For these themes see works of Bauman, Virno, Hardt and Negri—mentioned above.

13  *Democracy Inc., the Specter of Inverted Totalitarianism* (2008)

14  My own experience very much confirms this: I was among the protesters coming up 8th Avenue in New York past Madison Square Garden, in 2004, where the Republican Convention was taking place; coming up to 34th Street we confronted a phalanx of mounted police who shunted us right on 34th, keeping us from ascending toward Central Park, to the great lawn where a rally (which meanwhile has been banned—to protect the grass or for some other similar 'reason') was originally supposed to take place. Elsewhere that day a 'police riot' took place; hundreds of demonstrators were arrested, many beaten, then held just long enough to prevent further demonstrating.    Years later the demonstrators were exonerated from wrongdoing.

15  We won't be missing the rat infested, junky and drunk filled space the city had allowed it to become—surely *so* we wouldn't miss it (too much)—before it was privatized; but what about Madison Square, at 23rd and Madison, once an edenic, pastoral space, currently being gobbled up by an upscale Hamburger stand (what's not become an outdoor art gallery)? On the disappearance of public space see Passavant "Postmodern Republicanism", 7; Hardt and Negri, 187-88; certainly also throughout the work of Mike Davis, for instance, "Fortress Los Angeles: the Militarization of Urban Space".

16  Marx and Engels, *Basic Writings*, "Theses on Feuerbach" (III), p. 244.

# I.    The Mirror Stage: *Thérèse Raquin*

1  *Simulations*: 151-52.

2  *Le Naturalism au théâtre*: 11, 24, my trans.

3  Commenting recently (*Artforum*, Summer 2010, p. 137)) on René Pollesch's production of *Mädchen in Uniform—Wege aus der Selbstverwirklichung* (Girls in Uniform—Ways Out of Self-Realization) at the Deutsche Schauspielhaus, Hamburg, of February, 2010.

4.  *Thérèse Raquin*: iii, my trans.

5  *Le Naturalism au théâtre*: 20; and surely Zola would have thought what Manet and Monet represented in painting.

6  Who is faulted for not having made the concessions necessary to have his work accepted by the Salon; the painter is a composite portrait, in which Claude Monet and especially Paul Cezanne figure very prominently.    Zola's fictional Cassandra prognosis about the latter's dim prospects turned out to be unwarranted (in the long run), if understandable, as Cezanne won his belated case around 1900 (by way of dealers, who apparently were creating taste, not only manipulating and exploiting it, another mistake of the novel), never having, after all to accommodate the 'museum' conservatism of the Salon.

7  *Le Naturalism au théâtre*: 27, my trans.

8  In his preface, an early and significant statement on literary naturalism, to the second edition of *Thérèse Raquin* (novel), after defending his work against the familiar litany of moralistic accusations (obscenity, pornography etc.), Zola wonders why no one thought to criticize it from the valid point-of-view of the exceptionality of the events that there transpire, even formulating such a reservation in the voice of presumed critic: "'*Thérèse Raquin* is a study of too exceptional a case; the drama of modern life is more flexible and not so hemmed in by horror and madness.    Such cases should be relegated to a subsidiary position in a book.'" [26]

9    "[James] Frazer [in *The Golden Baugh*] established also that often the old god, when
     sacrificed in this way, and perhaps because of the taboos which were laid upon him,
     appeared to carry away with him sickness, death and sin, and fulfilled the role of an
     expiatory victim and scapegoat." [Hubert and Mauss, p.5]
10   See Appendix 1, "Rewriting Naturalism: Émile Zola's *L'Assommoir* and Charles Reade's
     *Drink*."
11   Reade, p.34.


## II.    The Return of the Repressed: *Ghosts*

1    I think, for example it makes as much, if not more sense, to read his novel *L'Oeuvre* in
     terms of the persona's (Zola's, very clearly) limitations in his ability to understand the
     idealist's (Paul Cezanne) extremist modernism, than in terms of the latter's unwillingness
     to throw a sop to the Salon; all the more so since Cezanne, 'sticking to his guns', was
     eventually recognized, by art dealers (who also Zola evidently underestimated) even
     before the museums caught on.
2    "Predictably, puritanical critics responded with outrage to Ibsen's discreet reference to
     Oswald's inherited disease."[John Gassner, Preface to *Ghosts*, in Ibsen, p.69].   Outrage
     was not in short supply in England, where the play was produced there in 1891, at the
     Independent Theatre, which had been founded there by the naturalized Dutchman, Jacob
     T Grein, on the 'experimental' model of André Antoine's enormously important Théatre-
     Libre of Paris (the production of *Ghosts*, there, interestingly, seemed to shock no one, but
     to bore many...); not only the play was savagely attacked but also its authors and the
     theatergoers, who, for instance, according to Shaw (who quoted at length, hilariously
     from the British press of the time in his brilliant little study, *The Quintessence of
     Ibsenism*), were described as: "Lovers of prurience and dabblers in impropriety who are
     eager to gratify their illicit tastes under the pretence of art." [46], while, according to
     Grein the first performance of *Ghosts* "...elicited no less than five hundred articles,
     mostly vituperating Ibsen..." [Waxman, 214].
3    Interestingly he serves as a scapegoat for a modern critic (Gassner, in *Ibsen*, op. cit.), who
     blames him for burning down the orphanage: "When, because of the carelessness of a
     drunken carpenter, the orphanage has burned down completely...Ibsen has the carpenter
     himself propose to build a tavern in a red-light district..." [pp. 69-70]; however it's clear
     at the beginning of Act III that it was through Mander's carelessness (in disposing of a
     match) that the orphanage burned down, Engstrand subsequently exchanging his silence
     for funds to start his 'seaman's home'.
4    To cite, unavoidably, Conrad citing Marlowe citing Kurtz, in *Heart of Darkness*, where
     what's horror in Africa stays in Africa, Marlowe emblematically hiding it from the prying
     eyes of the Belgian fiancé who had asked about K's 'last words'!   Jameson, who,
     symptomatically, alerts us to a certain structural hypocrisy of the naturalist audience, is
     worth citing here too: "...the analogous [J. has been talking about the 'fearful futures'
     imagined by such as Philip K. Dick in his novel *Time Out of Joint*] terror of an older
     naturalism—was class based and deeply rooted in class comfort and privilege.  The older
     naturalism let us briefly experience the life and life world of the various underclasses,
     only to return with relief to our own living rooms and armchairs..." (*Postmodernism*, 286)


## III.   The Nature of the Beast: *The Power of Darkness*

1    It was performed, in French translation, in André Antoine's Théâtre Libre, in Paris, in
     1888, where it was very well received.
2    Wachtel, introducing Tolstoy's *Plays: Volume Two*: x.

3   Tolstoy is notorious for his dislike of Shakespeare, whose intensity it seems to me he so often matches—I'd guess because the latter often presents evil without necessarily moralizing it...

4   I am using the later translation, *The Realm of Darkness*, for citation, since language is more current.

5   "The specific intellectual and mystical attempts at salvation in the face of these tensions [related to the 'realm of scarcity'] succumb in the end to the world dominion of unbrotherliness. On the one hand, their charisma is *not* accessible to everybody. Hence, in intent, mystical salvation definitely means aristocracy; it is an aristocratic religiosity of redemption. And, in the midst of a culture that is rationally organized for a vocational workaday life, there is hardly any room for the cultivation of acosmic brotherliness, unless it is among the strata who are economically carefree. Under the technical and social conditions of rational culture, an imitation of the life of Buddha, Jesus or Francis seems condemned to failure for purely external reasons." [Max Weber, 357]

## IV.   The Dialectic of the Master and the Slave: *Miss Julie*

1   The deprived childhood of Thérèse is, however a significant element in the novel that didn't really make it into the play. In Ibsen's *Ghosts* the furthest back we go in the etiology of a character's behavior would be early adulthood, which is why, as limited as they are, they seem more autonomous as individuals than the automatons Strindberg creates.

2   Later he more than dabbled in alchemy, mysticism, psychotic paranoia. Cf. his strange novel, *Inferno*. Muray describes him arriving [mid 1890's] in Paris, an "atheist, naturalist, positivist...a Darwinian and Nietzschean, he reads *Seraphita* [Balzac's 'mystical' novel], then plunges into the mysteries." (210, my trans.)

3   I first saw it performed, very effectively for me, in a coffee-shop in West Philadelphia, in 1959.

4   "...the theatre is an experiment...a trial run in which are measured the real chances for the intervention of freedom in the world—whether it punish the proud man with an eternal torture or a terrible penance, as in the case of Prometheus or Tamerlaine, or it discover unknown regions that one only enters only in fear and trembling." [Duvignaud, p. 582, my trans.]. I should add, that, Duvignaud's examples being from the classical age of the free-willing subject, *freedom* here I think would be that of Strindberg's, that of Prometheus bringing fire (light) in 'experimentally' describing characters totally deprived of it, a gift to be 'punished' later by being chained to the rock (of paranoia) etc.? See note 2, just above.

## V.   The War Between the Classes: *The Weavers*

1   *The New Moral World*, #25, December 13, 1844 [Marx and Engels, Vol.4, pp.230-31].

2   *The Northern Star*, #346, June 29, 1844 [Marx and Engels, Vol. 3, pp. 530-34].

3   "*Das Blutegericht* [blood-sentence, meaning death sentence, passed on the workers by the classes who rule them], which was popular among Silesian weavers on the eve of the revolt" [Marx and Engels, translator's note, Vol. 3, p. 596]. Hauptmann changed the name of the song to *Dreissiger's Song*, after the manufacturer [see next note] whose house and property the rebels sack in the play.

4   From Engels' earlier account [Note 2, just above] it's clear that, for him, the Weavers were attacking the system of private property, not trying to obtain some: "The people in the meantime, entirely demolished the dwelling house of Mr. Zwanzinger [manufacturer,

called *Dressinger* in the play], and proceeded then to the warehouse, where they destroyed all books, bills of exchange and other documents, and threw the cash they found, amounting to upwards of 1,000 pounds [English] upon the street..." [Marx and Engels, Vol. 3, p.532].

5    *Vorwärts!* #60, August 7, 1844 [Marx and Engels, Vol. 3, p. 201]

6    In *The Weavers*, Old Hilse rejects proletarian violence for religious reasons; but this is clearly meant to be symptomatic of the way this "opium of the people" works within an oppressed class to contain revolutionary ferment as much as an expression of the character's individuality; for instance the weaver described above by Engels, in Hübner's painting, pointing to heaven, would be saying thereby: "that's whose concern it is to even things up!".

7    No Social Reform here, to get out or obtain the vote etc.

8    "The proletarian movement, which, from the Silesian riots, the weavers' battle as it is called, in June, 1844, has spread all over Germany..." [Engels, writing in *The Northern Star*, of London, September 13, 1845, cited in Marx and Engels, Vol. 4, p. 646]. That *The Weavers* was still 'political dynamite' fifty years later is evidenced by the fact that "Simmel decries government restrictions upon Berlin performances of Gerhart Hauptmann's "The Weaver" [sic]" (Frisby, 20, citing an article about the play by G. Simmel, of 1892)

9    But mostly written by Marx: "The Bauer brothers and their fellow thinkers announced that the sole active element in the world-historical process was their own theoretical activity, to which they gave the name of 'Critical Criticism' "! [Tatyana Yeremeyeva, "Preface" to Marx and Engels, Vol.4, p. xvi]

10   Waxman, p. 184-185.

11   Thematic in Marx, of course is the idea that the Communist revolution would liberate the Capitalist as well as the worker.

12   Fúrst and Skrine, 66, who mentions that Lenin himself supervised the Russian translation...


## VI.   In the Country of the Blind: *The Lower Depths*

1    See Appendix 2, "Awakenings".

2    Which it's said, later in the play, she 'runs away from', thus making it not impossible for audience to believe she has joined Peppel in Siberia, playing Sonia to Raskolnikov. In conversation with me after an excellent production of the play by Resonance Ensemble (NYC, June 2004, directed by Eric Parness), James T. Ware, who played Peppel, said he agreed with me in principle; but that even in the unlikely event such were to happen, Peppel would be unable or unwilling to change, Natasha ending up miserably unhappy still...

3    if not for the actors in Renoir's film version, The lovers do not elope, however, in Akira Kurosawa's version of 1957, more faithful to the original. Parenthetically, maybe for reasons of cultural context, plus the nature of the medium of cinema that has never been very welcoming toward the figure of the sage (I guess because they don't 'do' enough), Renoir and Kurosawa foreground the character of the lover-thief, Peppel (Jean Gabin, Tishuro Mifune), rather than that of the mystic wanderer, meditator and mediator, Luka, who seems to me to be the focus for Gorky, Brechtian *avant la lettre*.

4    Luka being obviously on the run from something; that he's not anxious to say what it is doesn't make him any more willing to talk to the law.

5    According to Jacques Chwat, introducing an English translation of the play, paraphrasing a letter Gorky wrote, but never sent, to Tolstoy about the time of the latter's death (1910), this admiration was likely not reciprocal. In this letter he explained the puzzling character of Luka: "...mention had been made of the fact, never quite confirmed or denied by Gorky, that Luka had been modeled in part on Tolstoy.... This letter may have been

written in answer to Tolstoy's view of Luka as unsympathetic and not believable. Since their meeting in 1900 Gorky regarded Tolstoy as his spiritual father, and they engaged in frequent polemics on religion notwithstanding the fact that Gorky was an avowed nonbeliever...." [Gorky, p. 17]

6    See "The Splendors and Miseries of Platonism in Three Russian Symbolist Plays of the Early Twentieth Century"; and for a literary genealogy of the figure of the Outsider, "Shakespeare's *King John*: Anguish of the Early Modern Subject", in my *Play of the World*, now in preparation.

7    This seems to me to be a or the central statement of the play, well articulated in the Renoir film version, but curiously missing from the otherwise more faithful Kurosawa; this is also  very close in mood to the idealistic (and maybe Romantic, see Sereni in Works Cited) early Marx, for instance the famous (and notorious) praise of man (by way of the rejection of religion) of the Feuerbach-imbued "Introduction to Contribution to the Critique of Hegel's *Philosophy of Law*": "*Man makes religion, religion does not make man. Religion is the self-consciousness...of man who has either not yet found himself or has already lost himself again. But man is no abstract being encamped outside the world. Man is the world of man*, the state, society....Religion is the *opium of the people.*" [Marx and Engels, Vol. 3, p.176.]

8    Original text of Marx: "Where, then is the *positive* possibility of German emancipation? *Answer*: In the formation of a class with *radical chains*, a class of civil society which is not a class of civil society, an estate which is the dissolution of all estates, a sphere which has a universal character by its universal suffering and claims no *particular right* because no *particular wrong* but *wrong generally* is perpetrated against it; which can no longer invoke a *historical* but only a *human* title; which does not stand in any one-sided antithesis to the German state; a sphere, finally, which cannot emancipate itself without emancipating itself from all other spheres of society and thereby emancipating all other spheres of society, which, in a word, is the *complete loss* of man and hence can win itself only through the *complete rewinning of man*. This dissolution of society as a particular estate is the *proletariat*." [Marx and Engels, Vol. 3, p. 186]. This emphasis I'm puttting on the Early Marx, it should be added goes against the drift of a powerful current of recent French thought on the matter, that identified with Louis Althusser, who dismissed the work(s) of Marx before *Capital*, as romantically humanist, preliminary to the 'rupture' (break) represented by the 'materialism' of the later work. Althusser points out, for instance, that Marx (and Engels) never published the work, from which 'idealistc' statements like the above are excerpted.   For a convincing and comprehensive counterargument (really a counterattack, its stated 'raison d'être') to Althusser's Marx, cf. Michel Henry, *Marx*, who sees Marx 'of a piece', and so in a more unitary way, remarking that Marx and Engels very much wanted to publish this work, but were prevented by editorial refusals and delays; Henry citing also Marx later correspondence, when he was well launched into his supposedly 'materialistic' phase, for very positive allusions to the early work (Henry 19-31). Of courses I'm not taking a position on any Real Marx, whether the humanist of Henry or the post-or anti-humanist of Althusser; just observing that the early Marx seems to more harmonious with the early naturalism of such as Zola, Strindberg, Tolstoy, Gorky Synge, Shaw, Ibsen and even Wesker—where individuality, albeit threatened does endure; whereas the later materialistic Marx of Althusser's structuralism, whereby the individual is swallowed up, formed, determined and (in the plays at least) squelched by compulsive systems of mass society would rather go along better with the 'hypernaturalism' (Lehmann's term, for theatre of such as Schwab, Fassbinder, Kroetz etc...cf. my p.1 ff.) deployed here for the theatre of Brown and Storey...

9    From the powerfully iconoclastic section "The Power of Money". [Marx and Engels, Vol. 3, pp. 322-26]

10  Cf. Janelle Reinelt's essay, "Theorizing Utopia: the War Plays of Edward Bond", grounded in Paul Ricoeur's *Lectures on Ideology and Utopia* for a progressive interpretation of the theme of utopia, as conveyed by this often grimly naturalist dramatist. Utopias, as seen through the lens of sci-fi, in Frederic Jameson's monumental interpretive survey of the genre: *Archaeologies of the Future: the Desire Called Utopia and Other Science Fictions*, as are the 'fantasies' of science fiction, are more about ideologies and representations of the present than the future. Additionally, Jameson is careful to allow for a totalitarian potential in Utopia, since one person's paradise is another's hell, even a 'democratic' one (as in Tocqueville's ominous theme of the "tyranny of the majority", already well in evidence in 1830 here, in *Democracy in America*). The classical utopias, Plato's and More's, have indeed frequently been thought of in totalitarian terms, Plato's *Republic* sometimes being denounced even for its fascist aspect, while More's *Utopia* surely was the very model of a system George Sorel thoroughly mistrusted: "Utopias, for Sorel, are inherently reactionary, insofar as they offer a guide to the perfect society in the name of which popular forces can be subject to technocratic and authoritarian designs." (Shapiro 302). In this sense it is certainly salutary that Luka doesn't stay around to guide the world he has been informing and reforming.

11  It was an ominous, perhaps reactionary, moment then, when the alcoholic Actor, deluded by Luka's stories, starts saving his kopecks in order to go to the nonexistent hospital.

12  Actually the last paragraph of the "Power of Money" section, cited above; quoted memorably by E. Fromm in *The Art of Loving* (p. 27), combining (early) Marx and Freud, as a basis for a (sick)-society-redeeming concept of psychotherapy.

# VII. A Living Like Any Other: *Mrs. Warren's Profession*

1  *Bernard Shaw*, p. 42.
2  see Chapter II, note 2.
3  ibid.
4  *Shaw's Complete Plays with Prefaces*, III, p. 22.

# VIII. A Naturalist Symbolism: *Riders to the Sea*

1  Synge, p. 11; her penultimate speech. First elision Synge's.
2  A distinct and significant offshoot of naturalistic theatre was (eventually) the disappearance, or at least submergence of character in the theory and practice of Italian postwar neo-realistic cinema—where History and Setting become all important, and, theoretically at least, the non-actor—that is, the audience—comes into its own. Cesare Zavattino, one of the formost spokesman of this movement, insists that "It is evident that with neorealism, the actor—as a person fictitiously lending his own flesh to another—has no more right to exist than the 'story'. In neorealism, as I intend it, everyone must be his own actor." (Zavattino, p.227). Edgar Morin, on the other hand, has shown how such a development, though philosophically consistent, tends to run counter to the demands of the capitalist culture industry, which creates individualized stars as marketable commodities and as escape valves for the frustrations and dreams of its exploited (as producers *and* consumers) masses: "Pushed to its limit realism tends to eliminate the star altogether (the neo-realist Italian movies). But this limit is rarely attained, precisely because the film remains within the framework of the middle-class version of the imaginary." (Morin, p. 21).
3  Pierre Mayol, p. 217 (citing Bernard Dort)
4  As in M.H. Abrams calling Romanticism "Natural Supernaturalism"!

5    On the advice of Yeats, Synge spent some time on the Aran Islands in 1901, an
     experience which was the basis both of the 'authenticity' of *Riders* and of a book
     composed that same year, *The Aran Islands*, and published in 1907, or after his play had
     aroused interest in and curiosity about 'the real place'.  In the play, the cottage, its
     interior and furnishings, the life style and routines of its inhabitants are all based on
     Synge's close personal observation.  It's not irrelevant also that Synge (as a matter of
     fact, like Shaw), was an early enthusiast of the 'naturalist' art of photography, having
     taken many pictures in the Aran Islands.
6    Which seems to be an original, and very rhythmical mixture of Gaelic and English we
     could almost call "Syngese"; cf. Saddlemyer, "Introduction", in Synge, p. xi.
7    Not as much of a sacrifice as it sounds, since, anyway, in fact the 'love' has already
     started to cool a bit, ineluctable effect of time, and will certainly continue to cool even
     further as the lovers age.  Actually the decision 'to die' is by then as thoroughly
     Symbolist as it sounds, following very closely the famous 'renunciation' of the lovers in
     Villiers de L'Isle Adam's *Axel's Castle*, published in 1890: "as for living, our servants
     will do that for us"!
8    It must be recalled that Synge had just about as little patience with God and religion as
     Joyce; although, apparently the two Irish authors did not get along, perhaps because the
     latter would of course have rejected Synge's recourse to Irish nationality and ethnicity,
     which Joyce, the internationalist, was of course much more ambivalent about.  More or
     less discreet or parodying allusions to Synge, and 'what he stood for' (Irish Revival,
     Gaelic, Abbey Theatre etc.) abound in *Ulysses* and *Finnegans Wake*.
9    *Riders* has in fact been turned into an opera, by Ralph Vaughan Williams.
10   God's existence, according to Pascal, cannot be proven or disproved; so believing,
     according to him, is the better option, affording us everything to gain, and nothing to
     lose.

## IX.   Living History: *Chicken Soup With Barley*

1    *The Plays of Arnold Wesker*, Vol. 1: by "all these plays" is certainly meant first of all the
     trilogy deploying essentially the same 'family' characters (as they age, develop, decline
     etc.) comprised of *Chicken Soup*, *Roots* (1959) and *I'm Talking About Jerusalem* (1960).
     Not quite family but yielding nothing in raw Naturalism to the *Chicken Soup* trilogy are
     two very important (and successful) other plays of Wesker from the same period, *The
     Kitchen* (1959), where all the action takes place as a 'day in the life' of the kitchen of a
     large restaurant, complete with preparing and dishing up 'real food'—Wesker drawing on
     his own experience working in the kitchen of a Paris restaurant; then *Chips With
     Everything* (1962), set in military barracks...
2    "Leah Wesker is best portrayed in the trilogy, where her character, Sarah Kahn,
     represents a mélange of quintessentially female traits....At once she is an articulate and
     feisty spokesperson for her political principles; a dedicated mother who sits tirelessly by
     her children's side when she is needed; an impatient, sometimes nagging wife of a
     misdirected but gentle tailor..." (Dornan, 114)
3    *Plays of Arnold Wesker*, Vol. 1, p. 149.
4    *Their Very Own and Golden City*, in *Plays of Arnold Wesker*, Vol. 2, p. 80
5    *Plays of Arnold Wesker*, *Vol.* 1, p. 136.
6    Trying to make sense of the life one has lived in the shadow of one's approaching end is
     very much of a factor in another play of Wesker's, *The Old Ones*, of 1972, which Wesker
     says is about "defiant old age".  However the most naturalistically 'faithful' description
     of dying in Wesker's work is not in one of his plays (where there are structural limits to
     how grim things can get), but is certainly the novella "Love Letters on Blue Paper", a
     kind of rewriting or reworking, with a bit of an added dimension of the trials of a best

friend and a wife confronting the situation, of the horrifying realism of Tolstoy's great "The Death of Ivan Illich."

7    Guy Debord's paraphrase of Marx; see p. 42, and Chapter VI, note 8, above for fuller excerpt and Marx original.

8    *Plays of Arnold Wesker*, Vol. 1, p. 76.

9    I am reading him, I gather from his website, against himself; Wesker certainly wouldn't like being described thusly: he would reject the label "Naturalist", for him, I'm sure insufficiently 'spiritual', even more so "revolutionary"...

10   Come to think of it, the savage inhumanity of the 'drilling scenes', turning men into robots by treating them as such, in the military play, *Chips With Everything* (1962), rendered with chilling naturalist authenticity, certainly shows that the lower classes have nothing to lose by shaking things up a bit!

11   *Plays of Arnold Wesker*, Vol. 1, p. 133.

12   See Solzhenitsyn, *passim,* who finds the attraction based on a number of factors: the Bolsheviks offered Jews an end to their timeless pariah status, a homeland at a time when Israel wasn't yet very much of a reality; in the fact that Judaism traditionally professed the ideal of justice on earth, it was led to defend a revolution that seemed to promulgate this; while that Judaism was monotheist and Communism atheist would seem to militate against this connection, for Solzhenitsyn—who nevertheless allows that secularism was far advanced by the time among Russian Jewry, *a fortiori* we may assume among the class-conscious Jews of London's East End, as Wesker describes them at the time; and then, Communism has often been described as a 'secular religion'!

13   *Plays of Arnold Wesker*, Vol. 1, p. 133

14   *Ibid*, p. 134.

15   *Ibid*, p. 141.

16   Wesker, like Orwell had served his down and out time there.

17   *Ibid*, p. 215.

18   See above, p.9; Marx and Engels, "Theses on Feuerbach", p. 244; not however published in Marx's lifetime. Marx was correcting Feuerbach's determinism. These "Theses" were written about the same time, middle 1840's, as Marx (and Engels) were realizing that the proletariat could (and was obliged to) take matters in their own hands....

19   *Plays of Arnold Wesker*, Vol. 1, p. 349.

20   *Ibid*, p. 352.

21   Jacques Rancière's comment on the effect of the disappearance of proletarian consciousness on the cinema of Ernst Lubitsch I think would explain why Naturalism was eventually phased out of the theatre of Wesker: "When the class struggle is no longer a factor ("derrière la porte"), when the End of History is proclaimed for all to hear....then social comedy invades the screen, gameplaying in family and society." My translation, Rancière, p. 156; quoted by the interviewer in *Traffic*, #50, "Les Écarts du cinéma".

22   For instance, on his website, which can be googled, where he celebrates Israel, hardly any home for an international proletariat...

23   Symbolically of course the kitchen and the way it's run are metaphors for the capitalist system and everything wrong with it; that same evanescence that, for Marx and Engels, is the essence of a capitalism that sweeps all permanence and traditions aside is the very quality of the kitchen for Wesker: "The world might have been a stage for Shakespeare but to me it is a kitchen, where people come and go and cannot stay long enough to understand each other, and friendships, loves and enmities are forgotten as quickly as they are made." ("Introduction and Notes for the Producer", *Plays of Arnold Wesker*, Vol. 1, p.3)

## X.    Living Theatre: *The Brig*

1    The author called it, rather than a play, a "concept for theatre or film", in its book
     publication.  *The Brig*, still directed by Judith Malina, was in recent (opened, August,
     2007) production by the Living Theatre at its new home on Clinton Street in the Lower
     East Side (Manhattan) where it had an extended run.
2    The theme of the military as incarnating the totalitarian essence of modern society
     (whatever its liberal-democratic facade) has been most intensely broached in many works
     of the French thinker, Paul Virilio: for example, *Bunker archéologie* (1975), *L'Esthétique
     de la disparition* (1989) and *L'Insécurité du territoire* (1993), among others...
3    Jack Gelber, whom Kenneth Brown described (in an email to me of 3/13/07) as having
     been a good friend of his, and whose play *The Connection* (1959) was another signal
     production of The Living Theatre, as a matter of fact directed the New York production
     of Wesker's *The Kitchen*..
4    What's narrative for example about 90,000 human beings being volatilized in 9 seconds,
     unless, of course, from a happy seat from the plane that just dropped that story?  Not that
     stories, tragedies in fact, won't abound for those (all the rest of us, eventually) outside of
     Ground Zero!
5    The Mekas brothers (Jonas and Adolfas) film (available on Mystic Fire Video) of a
     Living Theatre performance of the play, which won the 1$^{st}$ prize in, significantly,
     *documentary* at the Venice Film Festival of 1964, runs only a little more than an hour—
     of course, *what* an hour!  In the email to me of  note 3, just above, the author said also
     that "Mekis's [*sic*] movie would have been longer, but he shot a lot of it on film that was
     later revealed to be damaged and captured no image at all."
6    I remember now, for instance, over a half a century later, as if it was yesterday, the shock
     of seeing a burly bully of a neighbor punch my rather frail father (in the belly, yet), about
     some doubtless trivial matter, a blow to which there was no reply; I prefer to think my
     dad (died in 1996), of course, did 'not fight back' because of cowardice but because he
     sensibly didn't want to risk further damage to himself that would compromise his ability
     to care for his family. Yet how *much*  that blow hurt (me) at the time!; how I wished he
     would rather have gone down fighting than teach his son that terrible lesson that mere
     survival is worth such humiliation.
7    Walter Benjamin, cited in Agamben's *Profanations* (100ff), was of this opinion;
     according to Agamben, Benjamin went far beyond the famous insight of Max Weber that
     Capitalism was a kind of secularized Christianity; for Benjamin Capitalism is another
     religion entirely, centered for Agamben on consumerism, whose keystone, proxy for the
     pilgrimage of Christianity and Islam, would be the grueling mass masochism of the
     hordes of tourists wandering the earth for what they cannot possibly find at home
     (Capitalism the savage god having sucked the home environment dry of all use-
     enjoyment-meaning value, for example replacing a corner store with a mall), or anywhere
     else, for that matter: "This is why tourism, in so far as it represents the central cult and
     altar of the capitalist religion is certainly the world's biggest industry, mobilizing every
     year more that 650 million people.  Nothing is more astounding than to realize how
     millions of ordinary people wind up inflicting upon themselves doubtless the most
     desperate experience they ever had to endure: the irrevocable loss of all use [of the world
     around them]..." (Agamben 2005:107, my trans.); more germane to *The Brig*, even eerily
     so, would be Agamben's holocaust analyses, for instance in *Homo Sacer: Sovereign
     Power and Bare Life*, whereby the holocaust, far from being the rare, if regrettable
     exception its memorialists as well as its deniers affirm it to have been, is the
     characteristic, representative and absolutely faithful reflection and anticipation of a
     system that, stripping people of all connections to others, except quantifiable ones ('vital
     signs'), returns humans to their bedrock essence of 'bare life', subject to exploitation
     and/or elimination, as would be species of noxious rodents or insects: Those of us who

have seen the film *Hotel Rwanda* will remember that the Hutus referred to the to-be-murdered Tutsis as "roaches"; while in *The Brig* the guards customarily address the prisoners as "lice"...

8   Even in our 'ordinary' perceptions we dramatize, of course, certain aspects of it, depending on our situation—noticing cars if we're looking to acquire one, maybe legs out of lust, or others using prostheses like canes if we're forced to rely on one...

9   I am speaking of its audience as I imagine it to have been in 1963, not at all the same as the one (I've been a part of) for the play, recently revived (see note 1, just above); strangely, and a bit disturbingly, to tell the truth, the play has been recommended by an important reviewer, Christopher Isherwood  as a tour-de-force of a  performance and production, and especially of interest *historically*, kind of as an exhibit in a cultural zoo: "...anyone with a serious interest in the history of American theater will want to see *The Brig* if only for that rare opportunity it provides to revisit a moment when theater was in the forefront of both aesthetic and political radicalism.  That moment is now long past..." The title of the review, even before perusal certainly sets the nostalgic mood!: "Keeping the Old Off Off Broadway Spirit Alive". (Isherwood 27 April 2007: Sect. E, Part 1, 1)

10  For instance, in Hauptmann's *The Weavers* (1892) the proletarian rebels will be dying for the Communist ideal of a classless society....

11  See p. 72, above.

12  For whom it's the face ("visage") of the other that calls out to us all; a fortiori, surely if that face is a face in pain, basically the face of a naturalist theatre, life being the seamy mess that it is, whose 'mission'  was to "look at things as they are"!

13  As in probably the most pathetic scene in world literature, Marmeledov's widow, recently evicted, lamenting and keening with her children on the sidewalk in Dostoevsky's *Crime and Punishment*.

14  That overthrowing the  "specifically political structures of power" will be the result (or precondition) of any real challenge to "relations of domination" is insisted on even by so conservative a thinker as Paul Ricoeur, whom no one has ever thought of as a Marxist: "...relations of domination, rising out of the regime of expropriation—private, collective or state—of the means of production, can only hold because they are recognized and guaranteed by institutions, which in turn are sanctioned, ultimately, by a political authority; this to the point that relations of domination of an economico-social sort cannot be changed except through the *transformation of the specifically political structures of power*, one which puts the seal of institutional approval on all technological, economic and social forms of the power of man over man." (Ricoeur, *Finitude et culpabilité: I* , 134, my emphasis and trans.).  Speaking of the monopoly or control over necessities, like food and shelter, as a basic way one group exerts power over another, Norbert Elias has commented similarly:  "Any 'economic' monopoly, of whatever sort, is directly  or indirectly linked to some other monopoly, without which it could not exist, a monopoly over the use of physical violence and the utilization of its instruments, whether only a secondary and decentralized monopoly over the possession of weaponry by a great number of people, or, under absolutism, a centralized monopoly over physical violence in the hands of a single individual." (Elias, *La Société des individus* : 82-83, my trans.)

15  There were different versions, depending on how much "reality" its original French (it was performed in France, at Antoine's Théâtre Libre in translation before Russian censors would allow its performance in Russia) and/or Russian audiences could stand.  In a grimly compelling recent New York revival of the play (Mint Theater Company, opened September 2007, directed by Martin Platt), the baby was 'crushed to death' below the stage, but very audibly whimpering as it expired.

16  Cf. the discussion above, p. 27ff, of the historical basis of Hauptmann's *The Weavers* (1892), in The Silesian Weavers Rebellion of 1840's; and its impact on Marx and Engels and *The Communist Manifesto* (1848).

17  Image suggested by Derrida's *Specters of Marx*.

18  I am focusing of course on the naturalist moment in its history, or what was naturalist about it; but of course this wasn't all The Living Theatre was about, far from it; Artaud's Theatre of Cruelty, for example, was even more prominent in its theory and practice. Ultimately we are probably dealing with some kind of blend with a play like *The Brig*, of Naturalism and Cruelty, as was surely for the case for another signal production of The Living Theatre we'll be commenting shortly, *The Connection*.

19  See note 9, just above; *The Brig*, recently brought back, is still extraordinary theatre, but no one is going to close the playhouse and chase The Living Theatre out of the land, because vested interests are threatened by it, as they were clearly in 1964. Its audience seems to be drawn to it the way visitors are to an especially interesting (and informative) exhibit in a zoo, maybe keeping the species of revolutionary drama alive in a non-revolutionary age, so, being optimistic about future prospects, a kind of sleeper...

20  This was how they were injecting themselves (inserting syringes definitely into arms, filled with I'm not sure what) in the movie version (dir. Shirley Clarke, 1961). Two friends of mine, Lionel Bloom and Marjorie Gamso, who had seen the play 'back then' confirm also that 'junkies' (actors playing the part) also circulated in the aisles during intermission, panhandling for a 'fix'! In the recent revival of the play of early 2009, to celebrate the Living Theatre's 50th anniversary, directed by Judith Malina who also acted in it, the syringes were all 'medical' (AIDS has come between then and now) plus all 'fixing' was either offstage ('reported' from bathroom, though I wasn't the only one who distinctly smelled marijuana in a waiting area coming from where the actors were preparing...) and there was no suggestion of panhandling junkies at the performance: a stirring evening of theatre, what with the fine jazz (Rene Mclean Quartet) and inspired acting, but I do agree with Isherwood's review "Behind Glazed Stares They Wait for a Fix", that the play could have nowhere near the impact it once it once did, given that drugs have become so routine, even mainstream: "Addiction and rehab are now regular stops on the circuit of celebrity culture, after all," essentially coming to the same conclusion as he did for the revival of *The Brig* of 2007: "...yesterday's daring sociology is today's documentary kitsch." (C7)

21  For instance, anyone (except maybe a terminally ill person) who announces an intention to "end it all" is surely asking to be talked out of it: i.e. give him/her a "reason to live"...

22  We are referring of course to Michel Foucault, specifically to his 'deconstructions' of the 'imprisoning' (*le grand enfermement*, beginning in the 18th century, inspired and enabled by the Cartesian rationalism of the 17th) institutions of modernity, whose purposes are strategic, economic and political, whether by (mental) asylum, hospital, school, factory. In connection with the world of *The Brig* how not think, for example of Foucault's *Discipline and Punish* (N.Y., 1977, orig. pub. as *Surveiller et punir*, Paris, 1975), a comprehensive analysis of the ways the prison system has developed as tool of social control and regimentation, its real 'face' behind its mask of reform or even 'protection of society'—a way of pushing dissidents back in line, with (as we see in *The Brig* when James Turner is dragged away) the booby-hatch available for those who slip between the cracks?

# XI.  "Like a Neutron Bomb of the Mind": A Digression on Stiegler

1  Bernard Stiegler will however go to great pains to stress that he is not trying to revive an "I" that would be distinct from society: before there can be a "me" there, of course, has to be an "us", which "I" never come even close to getting clear of—even becoming a hermit presupposing a society that allows that choice, and from which to escape. For Stiegler, as for Marcuse notably, it's a question of degree, of how much society can lift from the individual without damaging the me and itself. Marcuse, for example, talked frequently

of "excess oppression", in cardinal texts for the rebelling '60's like *One-Dimensional Man* and *An Essay on Liberation*. Following Marcuse also, Stiegler would however regard many of the hedonistic 'liberating' ways of the Sixties (turned into the 'tyranny of pleasure's' rights and duties today) as being rather a kind of "repressive desublimation" (Marcuse's language), controlled and programmed leisure that reinforces the hegemony of the consumer society rather than constituting any authentic expression of the individual. Stiegler would therefore, I think, not demur from such denunciations of this style of permissiveness and self-indulgence as declaimed in Christopher Lasch's *The Culture of Narcissism*, of 1979. The theme of an essay on Nietzsche's influence on the arts, by Barbara Stiegler, included in the catalogue for a recent exhibition of "Dionysian art" ("Dionysiac") at the Pompidou Museum in Paris, was similarly cautionary, in warning that artists who throw off all restraint are not being as faithful to Nietzsche as they think; for Nietzsche, according to her, the raw passionate, inchoate thrust of Dionysus needed to be balanced and limited by the forming and taming power of Apollonian reason.

2    Curiously, Stiegler came up challenging private property in a rather direct way: before he became an illustrious French philosopher he had a little career going, in his youth, in crime (armed robbery, burglary etc.), as a consequence of which, in the hallowed footsteps of François Villon, the Marquis de Sade and Jean Genet before him, he had served time in prison...

3    As confirmed to me by Steven ben Israel, who acted in them in 1963... This is not the case for the recent (opened August, 2007) production; both the author, Kenneth Brown and Steven ben Israel mentioned this would be because the guards have now been cast as perceptibly older than prisoners; reasonably this says something also about the less radical epoch we live in and a diminished role for theatre in it (politically, at least), as more than intimated by Isherwood in his review of the play (notes 9 and 19, for Chapter X, just above).

4    Stiegler has occupied a high administrative position in media matters in France, as a matter of fact as Director of The National Audiovisual Institute (1996-99).

5    Nor is Stiegler reviving the rampant ego-philosophy of Max Stirner, whose *The Ego and His Own*, of 1845, was very much in Marx's way when he was in process, at the same time, of formulating a social, therefore class-based revolutionary consciousness, turning for example vast swaths of *The German Ideology*, completed in 1846 (but not published until the 1930's) into a debate with Stirner. This antinomy, between the individual and society (and between Stirner and Marx), obviously too perpetual and undecidable to die, surfaces again quite centrally in Derrida's *Specters of Marx* (where he had much to say about Stirner, and the controversy that swirled around it too...)

6    This was written before the 'economic breakdown' of 2008-9, but I'd say whether the formerly 'better off' are ready to see themselves as proletarians (with nothing to lose but our chains) remains to be seen.

7    *Echographies of Television: Filmed Interviews of The National Audiovisual Institute.* Stiegler, along with Virilio (see Ch. X, n.2, above) is mentioned by Derrida in *Specters of Marx* (n. 36, p. 195) in the context of the ways in which technology needs to be considered in rethinking Marx today, in the interests of "a *new* concept of class and class struggle while taking more fully into account the new realities of the techno-scientifico-capitalist 'modernity' of world society." (Derrida, "Marx and Sons", 239).

8    *Hamlet* figures very prominently in *Specters of Marx*, where the *ghost* of the former's father = ghost of Communism, making analogous demands, as difficult to satisfy as to neglect.

9    As in our volunteer army, where the poor (who else would join up?) die in the wars of the rich (why else would they start them?)...

10   "...it is only through staking one's life that freedom is won." (Hegel 114), Relevant to what follows is the "Lordship and Bondage" section, pp. 111ff.

11 The shame I talked of feeling above(note 6, Chapter X) at my father 'not fighting back' maybe arose out of an instinctive grasp of this 'situation' long before I had ever heard of any master-slave dialectic!

12 Following Agamben on this point (*Ce Qui Reste d'Auschwitz*, passim), we quite agree that, after our last century or so of mass 'exterminations', this 'tragic' death or dramatic risk of it is ethically irrelevant, if not a piece of egregious effrontery: "The Greek hero has left us forever...after Auschwitz the tragic paradigm has become, for us, ethically useless" (*ibid*, 197, my trans.); however that which is ethically obsolete can still be politically and dialectically very powerful, even indispensable; or in the ringing words of Aldous Huxley: "Liberties are not given; they are taken." (quoted *passim* for instance in the late Howard Zinn's *Failure To Quit*, where the leitmotif was the necessity of actions of defiance of 'unjust' laws and Civil Disobedience to realize the rights inscribed in the U.S. Constitution and its amendments, especially The Bill of Rights, the first 10 and the 14th, on Civil Rights, which required the 'revolution' of the Civil Rights Movement to come anywhere near to actualizing...)

13 See my *Alchemy of the Word, Cabala of the Renaissance* (SUNY, 1998); and Gershom Scholem's *Sabbatai Sevi, Mystical Messiah* (Princeton, 1973).

# XII. On the Side of the Object: *The Contractor, The Changing Room*

1 "...like Wesker's *The Kitchen*, *The Contractor* seems to give working activities prominence over individuality and to let the substance of the plot be determined by the place. In fact both plays are naturalistic in the same sense as the best of Zola's novels." (Hayman, *British Theatre*, p.56)

2 "Notes on Naturalism: Truth is Stranger as Fiction", cited in Rosen, p. 15, originally published in *Performance 1* (March-April, 1973), pp. 34-39, where Kauffmann also emphasizes, acutely: "...naturalism now can be seen only through eyes conditioned by (historically) post-naturalist theatre." (p.37)

3 Rosen, pp. 15-16.

4 For instance an (older) rugby player in *The Changing Room* gets his nose bashed in (off stage, during the game), is lead in bleeding profusely, then sent off in an ambulance to hospital, it being apparent that this will be the end of his career, not that this was at all what the play was about; or, in *The Contractor*, there is a personality clash between a supervisor and a worker, with the result that the former fires the latter, but this dismissal is cancelled almost immediately, by the boss who shows up...

5 For instance, in *In Celebration* (1969), the three sons who come home to celebrate the anniversary of their parents marriage all represent divergent points-of-view (businessman son, artist son, borderline son) that are presented as the strict outcome of their circumstances, with none, finally being privileged—or any being anything but momentarily favored; or, even more excruciatingly, in *Home* (1970), which, dramatically (because not immediately) reveals itself to be a mental asylum, and the conversations of the actors those of the *mad*, it would be sheerer madness still to think in terms of right and wrong; as much of a novelist than a playwright, Storey's fiction tends to be more or less thinly disguised autobiography, with persona that match the age and situation of the writer throughout his career, but early on very much bildungsromans about his coming-of-age in a proletarian environment, where scruples had to be kept to a minimum, one with clear bridges, naturalistically to his theatre: *This Sporting Life* (1960), his first novel, was based on the author's rough-and-tumble rugby experiences, and links directly, of course to *The Changing Room*; while in a later novel, the protagonist, a clear persona of the author, works for a tent contractor, of the same name (Ewbank) as the one in *The Contractor*.

6     Deploying Mircea Eliade's theme of the 'desacralization' of modern secular culture, William Hutchings, in a book length study, *The Plays of David Storey*, has characterized his 'ordinary' settings (workplace, home etc.) as directed at a 're-ritualization' of everyday life; in another book on Storey's plays, by Herbert Liebman, *The Dramatic Art of David Storey*, the handling is rather less 'mystical', anchored in a theme of the dramatic overcomings of the alienations of modern life, as limned in the psychology and existential psychotherapy and psychoanalysis of Ronald Laing. Given the lack or even total absence of ideological statements in Storey (and/or the distinct irony with which he treats all such and the characters who make them), such starkly different takes on what he was up to are to be expected; not that the lack of ideology might not be an ideology in its own right, possibly not the least ideological one.

7     Liebman, p. 40ff, argues at length that the audience is not convinced, especially since, in a Laingian sense the conditions of his life have not changed.

8     Some of Storey's other plays were said to be, however meritorious, derivative, for instance *Home* clearly owing to Pinter, whose plays Storey, improbably, claimed never to have seen or even read, at the time of its New York opening, as reported by Guy Flatley, "I Never Saw a Pinter Play" (*New York Times*, Nov. 29, 1970, Sec. 2)

9     *Fatal Strategies*.

10    The reader will, by now, have understood that we could have chosen from many other authors, especially after the 'classical' beginnings of Zola, Antoine, Hauptmann, Ibsen, Strindberg, Gorky and Shaw—among so many others, Chekhov, O'Neill, Williams, Miller, Edward Bond, F.X. Kroetz, Peter Weiss, Davids Rabe and Hare, Odets (probably our least forgivable omission), Dürrenmatt, and most certainly Wallace Shawn, it being no indication of our judgment on the relative merit of the playwrights we have chosen to write about, for reasons having to do with issues we wanted to take up, and contrasts we wanted to make (for instance between the political naturalism of Wesker and the apolitical one of Storey) compared to ones we have omitted to consider. From a purely documentary perspective, anyway, we could not have avoided dealing with Eugène Brieux (1858-1932), whom Peter Skrine calls "The major force in French Naturalist drama...unquestionably....After Ibsen's death, he was ranked by Shaw as 'the most important dramatist west of Russia', and was generally regarded as the equal of Ibsen, Strindberg, Gorky, Chekhov and Hauptmann, the counterpart therefore in French Naturalist drama of Zola. But quite unlike these, he has subsequently lost his reputation entirely." (Fürst 61). Being still known and performed, or having been so within my (starting around 1950's) living memory, wasn't our only criterion, but it had to be a qualifying one, in attempting to keep this work lively and relevant; cf. also for the 'rationale' of our choices, and especially our 'radical' take on this theatre of naturalism, which has fitted in quite well also with 'bourgeois' ideology, above pp. 5 ff.

11    "aesthetic, poetic, symbolic" are adjectives commonly found accompanying the noun "naturalism", when critics discuss Storey; cf. Hutchings' *Casebook*, passim. The reader may recall we have described the theatre of Synge abundantly above also as a "symbolic naturalism", occurring, as is Storey's as a response to a certain exhaustion of political or revolutionary naturalism; but Storey's would be a symbolism of the objects, tools and sites of the present, whereas Synge conjures an ethnic symbolism of a haunting past, "revolution" not in a political sense, but in the sense of "revolving" or "come again".

12    My daughter, Céline, who served a 'stage' at a classy restaurant, in Paris, filled me in on the sexist aspect, fully an element in Wesker's version too!

13    Storey, *Home*, in *The Changing Room etc.*, p. 143.

14    Individuals in a class has been defeated politically (and/or economically and militarily), with little or no hope of throwing off its subjection to its rulers, seem to forsake solidarity as a class for competition with each other. So, for example, Norbert Elias' Marxist (and Freudian) analysis of the competitive rapports among the feudal nobility that, increasingly was being dominated by the royalty in the Renaissance would apply, I think,

very well to the working classes as represented in the theatre of David Storey, which life in the first decade of the 21$^{st}$ Century does very little to disconfirm: "Fear, born of the situation of the group as such, concerned with the maintenance of its superiority [over groups even lower], of the threat, more or less great that weighs on it, favors the strict observation of a code of behavior, and the development of a Superego. On the level of the individual this fear is expressed by anxiety over personal failure, and the loss of prestige in the eyes of other members of one's society." [*La Dynamique de l'Occident*, p. 212, my trans.] After the events the French Fronde of the 17$^{th}$ century surely the same internecine struggle, as depicted so vividly in the memoirs of Saint-Simon, was characteristic of the defeated nobility, all vying for their place in the Sun King's rays...

15    Storey, *The Contractor*, in *The Changing Room etc.* p. 158.

16    Haffenden, p. 277.

17    Cf. Chapter XI above *"A Neutron Bomb of the Mind"*, a Digression on Stiegler, where I take up the political implications of this denial of class (struggle) in Stiegler (and Derrida), retroactively with reference to *The Brig* .

18    "Naturalism's central category is milieu—the quintessence of everything alien to the individual and to which a hollow subjectivity must finally submit" (Szondi, p. 60); and, indeed, Storey's theatre is that *place* where milieu is everything, the subject becoming merely décor, where, as in Mallarmé's daunting phrase, "Rien n'aurait lieu que le lieu" ("Nothing would take place but the place"), a meeting of naturalism and symbolism justifying the eventual naming of Storey's style as that of a symbolic naturalism! But see note 11 above for a demarcation of Storey's from the symbolic naturalism of Synge. It should be further mentioned that  Szondi's view of naturalism in *Theory of Modern Drama* is not a sanguine one; for him, naturalistic drama was meant to deal with the impasse at which the theatre had arrived in bourgeois culture, where individuals had become isolated atomized entities with nothing to say to each other, each (soliloquizing, even in the 'presence' of the other) in their own monad of a world.  Naturalism's provenance in proletarian consciousness would have countered this by providing a basis for communication in class solidarity, which, when it turns out to be false, passé or a chimera (as in Storey's plays), that is when the working class starts conceiving itself as a bourgeoisie-in-the-making, has lost its purpose and its function: "The passage of the Drama from the aristocracy to the bourgeoisie in the eighteenth century corresponded to a historical process; the naturalist incorporation of the proletariat on [*sic*] the Drama circa 1900 was, on the other hand, an effort to evade history." (Szondi, p. 51)

19    Our idea of parody, excluding, at least in Storey, the ideological, would be closer to the 'value-free' neutrality of Jameson's concept of *pastiche* (*Postmodernism*, p. 16-19), characteristic, according to him of postmodern culture.  As Dürrenmat has observed ours is the age of Comedy , not that of Tragedy anyway, based on a concept of freedom of the will no longer tenable today.   Tragedy, therefore, if at all, would be feasible as the approach to it which would be *parody*, as in the Wooster Group's highly ingenious and technologically sophisticated version of *Hamlet* (Fall, 2007) production at the Public Theater in New York, where Richard Burton's famous TV-film version of the 1950's was the backdrop against which the play was reenacted...

20    The other edge, of course, of the film sword is the distortion, exaggeration and manipulation of reality, its Expressionist potential, which has made it an ideal medium for science fiction, futurism and fantasy generally.  For an account of this "debate" between Realism and Expressionism in film, which has been going on ever since its beginnings, see Malcolm Turvey, "Balàzs Realist or Modernist?"

21    Ex-Senator Bob Dole's erections, for example, heavy shelling in the first, beach-clearing barrage of Viagra commercials, early in this century....

22    The theme of the traditional insulation, now a very porous one, of the audience from the sufferings being staged, is a leitmotif in Samuel Weber's *Theatricality as Medium*.

23  *Ibid*, pp. 331ff, where Weber reads Baudrillard's provocative (Americans "brought it on
    themselves, wished it, dreamt about it before it happened etc.") essay on 9/11, first
    appearing in *Le Monde* of 11/3/01 through Debord's *Society of the Spectacle*,
    Baudrillard's analysis making sense, for Weber, only if America is conceived to have
    become a Society of Spectators. To throw my own ineluctable two cents in this stew,
    myself, I watched the 'events' on TV just across the river, with a class, in Brooklyn,
    thinking, at first, it was only a show; then found myself rushing with the crowds that were
    streaming over the Brooklyn Bridge, trying to outrace the cloud that was spreading by
    that time over us all: first you see it on TV then you're running from it for your life: TV
    as Smoke Alarm!

24  Cf. *The Conspiracy of Art*.

25  "The essence of the theatrical operation is the convocation of an audience, and every
    representation is a new convocation....Theatre as such is powerfully archaic, since it
    alone among the arts escapes reproducibility... " (Bailly, p. 67, my trans.). This
    existential quality links theatre on one side, Bailly adds, to religious ritual, while on the
    other side he considers theatre any spoken, sung (music generally, ostensibly) or dance
    modes "whose *meaning can be exerted* only only in the presence of an assembly which
    observes them    (listens, watches), gathered especially to see them *where they're
    performed*" (ibid, 68).

26  Musil (1880-1942), an amazingly prescient (like Cassandra not believed, in the sense of
    under-recognized)  and  profoundly  Nietzschean  author  who  has  anticipated,  to  a
    remarkable degree, much of this collapse of the subject into the object, in the context of
    an overwhelmingly anti-humanist technology, science and economy, as described by
    Baudrillard recently and expressed, the way I see it, by the evolution of naturalist theatre
    in the direction Storey has taken it, or has been taken by it.

27  Cf. S. Weber, p. 97ff. and passim; we disagree, however, emphatically with this author
    that theatre is intrinsically separated from politics, not only because it is often in the very
    thick of things, for instance, with Hauptmann's *Weavers*, dramatizing one of the first
    authentic proletarian rebellions, in a time of political unrest, or, in the days of Queen
    Elizabeth, the performance of *Richard II* (which almost cost Shakespeare his ears), with
    its suggestive deposition scene, out of sequence, on the night of the Essex rebellion, but
    because the very constitution of a place apart can be and often is and was political.  In
    many ways outright rebellion is easier for power to handle than indifference; ultimately,
    Christians, turning the other cheek, had more to do with the fall of the Roman Empire
    than the insurrectionary Jews... For the currency of current strategies of flight and exodus
    (in such as Paolo Virno, Antonio Negri and Michael Hardt), as opposed to direct
    confrontation, see above pp. 6ff.

28  For a critique-deconstruction of this philosophy and some of its current applications, for
    instance the concept of 'borderline psychotic' personalities who (try to) behave *as if*
    they're normal, cf. Giorgio Agamben, *Le Temps qui reste*, p. 64ff.; actually Agamben is
    scathing in his denunciation of a certain (sentimental) tendency to believe in the ideal as
    sufficient of itself to transform reality, with which we fully concur, seeing the 'as if'
    more as a tool and a role than anything essentially to go by or get by with; cf. also the
    strange notes left by Glen Freeman, gathered together in *Kryptadia*,  passim, for a
    brilliant exposition of the philosophy of Jules de Gaultier, or "Bovarism", after Mme.
    Bovary, that is the ineluctable human need and necessity to see ourselves as "other than
    we are"...

29  Cf. also "Madness, Theatre, Text", in our *I Am A Process With No Subject*, pp. 216-31;
    where we discuss the movements of author and reader into each others territory in
    "experimental" texts by such as Joyce, Beckett, Blanchot, and Des Forêts.

30  Jerzy Grotowski found "it is necessary to abolish the distance between actor and audience
    by eliminating the stage, removing all frontiers" (cited Turner, p. 52), thereby dissolving
    the audience by conflating it totally with the actor. Well, here, the goal in Grotowski's

approach evidently having something to do with the actors development (spiritual, mystical, psychological etc.?), as people they become their (only) own audience. In such a utopian (or dystopian) setting everyone becomes their own actor, no?, shedding of course a strange new light on Antoine Vitez' dream of "an elite theatre for everyone" (Sarrazac, *Critique du Théâtre*, 15, my trans.). A kind of outer limit of this disappearing act seems to be reached in the post-dramatic performance events of such as Heiner Goebbels's *Stifters Dinge* (December 2009, Park Avenue Armory, NYC), who gets rid of actors entirely, in that "strangely beautiful multimedia installation... 'a no man show', the director has jokingly called it...As Goebbels explains it, 'Even though there are no human bodies on stage, you could also say that the audience is the protagonist, sitting in the center of everything.'   Then he adds with mischievous glee, 'A lot of people tell me afterwards they are happy that, finally, there's no one on stage telling them what to think' " (Schwartz, p.33).   At least $55 a ticket, by the way; so lets keep our perspective here, this audience, actor-less or not (for a production sponsored by The Lincoln Center), with an family income which must be something like the $200,000 the New York Times reports for the average Broadway spectator, is not going to rush out and change things, not while they're not being drafted or too exorbitantly taxed; theatre being in the U.S., even more so apparently than in other 'advanced' countries (certainly in Europe where state funds so much of it) pretty much of a privileged class activity or outlet, or conspicuous consumption.   On the other hand the fact that the ruling classes keep it so well quarantined is perhaps a testimony to theatre's potential of subversion...  Then again more than mere numbers would be involved anyway in deciding  on the relative significance, or lack thereof, of theatre in our societies.   That audience, for example of Jean-Christophe Bailly (note 25, just above), if I understand him correctly, which *must* be convoked (since every theatrical event for him is a convocation) doesn't necessarily have to *be there* for there to be theatre.   There's such a thing as the saving grace of the audience "en attente", expected, just the fact that the 'people' may appear, one that must exist for it to be absent, "that symbolic and absent people, that utopian people....is absent, but it has been convoked, and every spectator by their presence contributes to the possibility of the coming...of an absentee, who is taken into account, who can come, who possibly will come. This could be anyone: that is to say, the people." (Bailly, 80-81, my trans.)   Coincidentally and amusingly relevant to this 'floating' of audience and performance is "A Theatre in Times Sq. With Seating For Just One" we read about in the New York Times of 5/14/10, where we make the acquaintance of the producer Christine Jones who in May of 2010 has scheduled six new plays and a dance for a run of 10 days in the theatre of a "movable box 9 feet long and 4 feet wide...in Times Square, weather permitting....Just as every performance will have only one audience member, every performance will have only one performer." (Barron )

31   As in a play, written by Mick Stern, *Audience* [Maria Flophaus Theater Company, performed June, 2006, New York City], where the actors are seated on stage waiting to be 'entertained' by the audience; or also, notably in Second City-type experimental theatre, and its offshoots, like the Playback Theatre (concept developed by Jonathan Fox), a branch of which I knew, through acquaintance with two of its principal 'actors', Tom and Kristen Bissinger, as the Playback Philadelphia Company, directed by Sarah Halley, where the material came directly from the audience, which then sees 'staged' its own fantasies, ideas, dreams, obsessions...

32   There are, and certainly have been, what we would call, strictly speaking, societies without theatre: Ancient Israel, for example; but I am thinking of theatre in more general sense of Pierre Legendre, who makes it practically synonymous with social existence itself: "A society is not just a lot of groups or a terrain for individuals but the theatre where we enact, tragically and comically, our reasons for living." (*La Fabrique de l'homme occidental*, p. 9, my trans.); or, if according to Jerome Rothenberg, alluding to

Victor Turner, "social conflicts are a form of theatre" (p. 13), then truly there is no society without theatre.

# Appendix

1    Sartre was indicting François Mauriac for ultimately granting by (divine) fiat to his characters a 'liberty' that his novel(s) made inconceivable: "Dieu n'est pas un artiste; M. Mauriac non plus" (end of "M. François Mauriac et la liberté," in *Situations I*.

2    Méténier was co-translator for Théâtre-Libre's production of Tolstoy's *Power of Darkness* (1888), rendering, apparently, Russian peasant language into Parisian street slang.

3    He had been secretary to the police commissioner [Chothia, p.88].

# Bibliography

Abirached, Robert. *La Crise du personnage dans le théâtre moderne*. Paris : Grasset, 1978.

Agamben, Giorgio. *Ce Qui Reste d'Auschwitz*. Trans. from Italian Pierre Alferi. Paris: Rivages, 1992.

———. *Homo Sacer: Sovereign Power and Bare Life*. Trans. Daniel Heller-Roazen. Stanford: Stanford University Press, 1998.

———. *Profanations*. French trans. Martin Rueff. Paris: Éditions Payot & Rivages, 2005.

———. *Le Temps qui reste: Un Commentaire de* L'Epitre aux Romains. Trans. Judith Revel. Paris: Rivages, 2004.

Althusser, Louis. *Pour Marx*. Paris : Maspero, 1965.

Bailly, Jean-Christophe. "Un Jour Mon Prince Viendra." *Le Théâtre, le peuple, la passion, Rencontres de Rennes*. Besançon: Les Solitaires Intempestifs, 2006: 61-82.

Barron, James. "A Theater In Times Sq. With Seating For Just One." *New York Times* 14 May 2010: A20.

Baudrillard, Jean. *The Conspiracy of Art*. Ed. Sylvere Lotringer. New York: Semiotext(e), 2005.

———. *L'Échange symbolique et la mort*. Paris: Gallimard, 1976.

———. *L'Esprit du terrorisme*. Paris: Galilée, 2002.

———. *Fatal Strategies*. Trans. Philip Beitchman and W.G.J. Niesluchowski. New York: Semiotext(e), 1990.

———. *Simulations*. Trans. Paul Foss, Paul Patton and Philip Beitchman. New York: Semiotext(e), 1983.

Bauman, Zygmunt. *Consuming Life*. Cambridge, UK: Polity Press, 2007.

———. *Wasted Lives: Modernity and Its Outcasts*. Cambridge, UK: Polity Press, 2004.

Beitchman, Philip. *Alchemy of the Word: Cabala of the Renaissance*. Albany: SUNY Press, 1998.

———. "The Empire's New Codes, Jean Baudrillard and 9/11", unpublished paper, available from author; presented at the $20^{th}$ and $21^{st}$ Century French and Francophone Studies International Colloquium, Minneapolis (Univ. of Minnesota), March 28, 2009.

———. *I Am A Process With No Subject*. Gainesville: University Press of Florida, 1998.

———. *The View From Nowhere*. Lanham: University Press of America, 2001.

———. "There Is No Walking in This Play". Introduction to Tom Bissinger: *Da Capo: Selected Writings, 1967-2004*. X-Libris, 2008: 11-24.

Bentley, Eric. *Bernard Shaw*. New York: New Directions, 1947.

Bissinger, Tom. *Selected Writings, 1967-2004*. X-Libris, 2008.

Blau, Herbert. *The Audience*. Baltimore: Johns Hopkins University Press, 1990.

————. *To All Appearances, Ideology and Performance.* New York and London: Routledge, 1992.

Bradshaw, Thomas. *Prophet.* New York: Samuel French, 2006.

Briusov, Valery. *The Wayfarer* (1910). Trans. Daniel Gerould. *Theater of the Avant-Garde, 1890-1950.* Ed. Cardullo and Knopf. New Haven: Yale University Press, 2001: 64-71.

Brown, Kenneth H. *The Brig.* With an essay, "Storming the Barricades", on The Living Theatre by Julian Beck and "Director's Notes", by Judith Malina. New York: Hill and Wang, 1965.

Chantraine, Pierre. *Dictionnaire étymologique de la langue grecque.* Tome 2. Paris: Éditions Klincksieck, 1970.

Chothia, Jean. *André Antoine.* Cambridge: Cambridge University Press, 1991.

Dahl, Mary Karen. *Political Violence in Drama : Classical Models, Contemporary Variations.* Ann Arbor : UMI Research Press, 1987

Davis, Mike. "Fortress Los Angeles: the Militarization of Urban Space". *Metropolis: Center and Symbol of Our Times.* Ed. Philip Kasnitz. New York: NYU Press, 1995: 355-68.

Debord, Guy. *The Society of the Spectacle.* Tr. Donald Nicholson-Smith. Zone Books: Brooklyn, 1995; orig. published as *La Société du spectacle.* Paris: Buchet/Chastel, 1967; Champs Libres, 1969.

Derrida, Jacques. "Marx and Sons." *Ghostly Demarcations: A Symposium on Jacques Derrida's* Specters of Marx. Ed. Michael Sprinker. London: Verso, 1999: 213-69.

————. *Specters of Marx: The State of Debt, The Work of Mourning and The New International.* Trans Peggy Kamuf. London and New York: Routledge, 1994.

Diederichsen, Diedrich. "Parables of the Theatre". *Artforum* XLVIII: 10 (2010): 137-40.

Dornan, Reade W. *Arnold Wesker Revisited.* New York: Twayne, 1994.

Duvignaud, Jean. *Les Ombres collectives, sociologie du théâtre.* Paris: PUF, 1973.

Elam, Keir. *The Semiotics of Theatre and Drama.* London : Methuen, 1980.

Elias, Norbert. *La Dynamique de l'Occident.* Trans. from German, Pierre Kamnitzer. Paris: Calman-Lévy, 1975.

————. *La Société des individus.* Trans. from German, Jeanne Étoré. Paris: Fayard, 1987.

Freeman, Glen. *Kryptadia.* Intro. Philip Beitchman; graphic design Ron Rozewski. Pottstown, Pa.: Tom Bissinger Editions Unique, 2005.

Frisby, David. "Introduction to the Texts." *Simmel on Culture.* Ed. Frisby and Featherstone. London: Sage, 1997.

Fromm, Erich. *The Art of Loving.* New York: Harper and Brothers, 1956.

Fuchs, Elinor. *The Death of Character: Perspectives on Theater after Modernism.* Bloomington: Indiana University Press, 1996.

Fürst, Lillian and Peter N. Skrine. *Naturalism.* London: Methuen, 1971.

Gamso, Marjorie. "Cover(t) Stories." *Footnotes, Six Choreographers Inscribe the Page.* Ed. Elena Alexander. Australia: G&B Arts International, 1998: 65-79.

*Ghostly Demarcations: A Symposium...* Ed. Michael Sprinker. London: Verso, 1999.

Gorky, Maxim. *The Lower Depths.* Trans. Alexander Bakshy, with Paul S. Nathan. New York: Avon Books, 1974.

Guénon, Denis. *Livraison et délivrance théâtre, politique, philosophie.* Paris: Belin, 2009.

Haffenden, John, ed. *Novelists in Interview.* London: Methuen, 1985.

Hardt, Michael and Antonio Negri. *Empire.* Cambridge: Harvard University Press, 2000.

Hayman, Ronald. *Arnold Wesker.* 2nd Edition. London: Heinemann, 1974.

————. *British Theatre Since 1955.* Oxford: Oxford University Press, 1979.

Hauptmann, Gerhart. *The Weavers.* In *Three Plays.* Trans. Horst Franz and Miles Waggoner. New York: Frederick Ungar, 1951.

Hegel, G.W.F. *The Phenomenology of Spirit.* Trans. A.V. Miller. Oxford: Oxford University Press, 1977.

Heiberg, Hans. *Ibsen, A Portrait of the Artist.* Trans. Joan Tate. Coral Gables, Florida: University of Miami Press, 1972

Henry, Michel. *Marx*. Paris: Gallimard, 1976.

Hubert, Henri and Marcel Mauss. *Sacrifice*. Trans. W.D. Halls. Chicago and London: University of Chicago Press, 1968.

Hutchings, Willeam. ed. *David Storey: A Casebook*. New York: Garland, 1992.

———. *The Plays of David Storey*. Carbondale: Southern Illinois UP, 1988.

Ibsen, Henrik. *Eleven Plays*. New York: Modern Library (Random House), n.d.

———. *Four Great Plays*. Trans. R. Farquharson Sharp. New York: Bantam Books, 1984.

———. *The Wild Duck and Other Plays*. Trans. Eva Le Gallienne. New York: Modern Library, 1961.

Isherwood, Christopher. "Behind Glazed Stares, They Wait for a Fix." *New York Times* 10 January 2009: C1, 7.

———. "Keeping the Old Off Off Broadway Spirit Alive." *New York Times* 27 Apr. 2007: F. Pt.1-1.

Jameson, Frederic. *Archaeologies of the Future: the Desire Called Utopia and Other Science Fictions*. London: Verso, 2005.

———. *Postmodernism, or the Cultural Logic of Late Capitalism*. Durham, N.C.: Duke University Press, 1991.

Kershaw, Baz. *The Radical in Performance: Between Brecht and Baudrillard*. London: Routledge, 1990.

Krikorian, Yervant H, ed. *Naturalism and the Human Spirit*. New York: Columbia University Press, 1944.

Laclau, Ernest, "Can Immanence Explain Social Struggles?". *Empire's New Clothes*. Ed. Paul Passavant and Jodi Dean. N.Y. and London: Routledge, 2004: 21-30.

Lasch, Christopher. *The Culture of Narcissism*. New York: W.W. Norton, 1979.

Legendre, Pierre. *La Fabrique de l'homme occidental*. Paris: Mille et Une Nuits, 1996.

———. *Leçons VII: le désire politique du Dieu—étude sur les montages de l'État du Droit*. Paris: Fayard, 1988.

Lehmann, Hans-Thies. *Postdramatic theatre*. Trans. Karen Jürs-Munby. London & New York: Routledge, 2006; orig. published in German, 1999.

Lewis, Tom. "The Politics of 'Hauntology' in Derrida's *Specters of Marx*." *Ghostly Demarcations: A Symposium...* Ed. Michael Sprinker. London: Verso, 1999: 134-167.

Liebman, Herbert. *The Dramatic Art of David Storey: The Journey of a Playwright*. Westport: Greenwood Press, 1996.

Marcuse, Herbert. *An Essay on Liberation*. Boston: Beacon Press, 1969.

———. *One-Dimensional Man*. Boston: Beacon Press, 1964.

Marx, Karl and Friedrick Engels. "Theses on Feuerbach." *Basic Writings on Politics and Philosophy*. Trans. Foreign Languages Publishing House, Moscow. Ed. Lewis S. Feuer. New York: Anchor Books, 1959: 243-45.

Marx, Karl and Friedrick Engels. *Collected Works*. Vol. 3, 1843-44. New York: International Publishers, 1975.

Marx, Karl and Friedrick Engels. *Collected Works*. Vol. 4, 1844-45. New York: International Publishers, 1975.

Mayol, Pierre. "Review of *Correspondence, 1925-35* of Theodor Adorno and Alban Berg." *Esprit* 11 (Nov., 2004): 216-19.

*Mimesis, Masochism & Mime: The Politics of Theatricality in Contemporary French Thought*. Ed. T. Murray. Ann Arbor: University of Michigan Press, 1977.

Moi, Toril. *Henrik Ibsen and the Birth of Modernism: Art, Theater, Philosophy*. New York: Oxford University Press, 2006.

Morin, Edgar. *The Stars*. Trans. Richard Howard. New York: Grove Press, 1960.

Muray, Philippe. *Le 19 siècle à travers les âges*. Paris: Denoël, 1984

Musil, Robert. *The Man Without Qualities*, Vol. 1 & 2. Trans. Sophie Wilkins and Ernst Kaiser. New York: Coward-McCann1954.

Nashe, Thomas. *The Unfortunate Traveler*. London: Penguin, 1974; orig. 1590's.

130 The Theatre of Naturalism

Pascal, Blaise. *Pensées*. Ed. Ch.-M. des Granges. Paris : Garnier, 1964.
Passavant, Paul. "Postmodern Republicanism." *Empire's New Clothes*. Ed. Paul Passavant and Jodi Dean. N.Y. and London : Routledge, 2004 : 1-20.
Peckham, Morse. *Beyond the Tragic Vision*. N.Y.: Brazillier, 1962.
*Playwrights Before the Fall: Eastern European Drama in Times of Revolution*. Ed. Daniel Gerould; pref. Dragan Klaic. Segal Center Publications, 2009.
Rancière, Jacques. "Entretien avec Jacques Rancière". *Critique*. janv.-fév., 05: 141-59.
Read, Alan. *Theatre and Everyday Life : An Ethics of Performance*. London : Routledge, 1993.
Reade, Charles. *Drink*. Unpublished typescript. Daniel Gerould, Program in Theatre, CUNY Graduate Center. New York.
Reinelt, Janelle. "Theorizing Utopia : Edward Bond's War Plays". *The Performance of Power : Theatrical Discourse and Politics*. Ed. Sue-Ellen Case and Janelle Reinelt. Iowa City : Iowa City Press, 1991 : 221-32
Ricoeur, Paul. *Finitude et culpabilité: I: L'homme faillible*. Paris: Aubier, 1960.
———. *Lectures on Ideology and Utopia*. New York: Columbia University Press, 1986.
Rosen, Carol. *Plays of Impasse: Contemporary Drama Set in Confining Institutions*. Princeton: Princeton University Press, 1983.
Rostagno, Aldo, Julian Beck and Judith Malina. *We, The Living Theatre*. New York: Ballantine Books, 1970.
Rothenberg, Jerome. "New Models, New Visions: Some Notes Toward a Poetics of Performance." *Performance in Postmodern Culture*. Eds. Michel Benamou and Carles Caramello. Madison: Coda Press, 1977.
Sarrazac, Jean-Pierre. *L'Avenir du drame*. Belval: Circe, 1981
———. *Critique du théâtre, de l'utopie au désenchantement*. Belval: Circe, 2009.
Sartre, Jean Paul. *Situations I*. Paris: Gallimard, 1947.
Schechner, Richard. "Interviews with Judith Malina and Kenneth Brown." *Tulane Drama Review* 8, 3 (1964): 207-19.
Schwab, Werner. *Holy Mothers*. In *German Plays 2*. Ed. Dodson and Tushingham. Trans. Meredith Oakes. London: Nick Hern Books, 1999: 1-39..
Schwartz, Stan. "The Pianos Man: Heiner Goebbels's Abstract Extravaganza..." *Village Voice*, Dec. 9-15, 2009: 33.
Serenyi, Paul. "Marx Romantique". *Europe* 900 (April, 2004): 111-29.
Shapiro, Kam. "The Myth of the Multitude". *Empire's New Clothes: Reading Hardt and Negri*. Ed. Paul Passavant and Jodi Dean. London: Routledge, 2004: 289-314.
Shaw, George Bernard. *Complete Plays, with Prefaces*. Vol. III. New York: Dodd Mead, 1962.
———.*The Quintessence of Ibsenism*. New York: Dover, 1994; orig. published, 1904.
Solzhenitsyn, Alexandre. *Deux siècles ensemble, Vol II: Juifs et Russes pendant la période soviétique, 1917-1972*. Trans. Anne Kichilov, Georges Philippenko et Nikita Struve. Paris: Fayard, 2003.
Sprinker, Michael, ed. *Ghostly Demarcations: A Symposium on Jacques Derrida's Specters of Marx*. London: Verso, 1999.
Steiner, George. *The Death of Tragedy*. New York : Knopf, 1968.
Stiegler, Barbara. "Dionysos à Condition: Le Couteau d'Apollon et l'Oreille d'Ariane." *Dionysiac* [Exhibition Catalogue]. Paris: Centre Pompidou, 2005. English trans. available at www.centrepompidou.fr.
Stiegler, Bernard. *Aimer, nous aimer: Du 11 septembre au 21 avril*. Paris: Galilée, 2003.
———. *De la misère symbolique: 1. L'époque hyperindustrielle*. Paris: Galilée, 2004.
———. *La technique et le temps: 3. Le temps du cinéma et la question du mal-être*. Paris: Galilée, 2001.

Stiegler, Bernard, and Jacques Derrida. *Echographies de la télévision: Entretiens filmés.* Paris: Galilée and Institut national de l'audiovisuel, 1996; English trans.: *Echographies of Television: Filmed Interviews.* London: Blackwell, 2002.

Stirner, Max. *The Ego and His Own.* Trans. Steven T. Byington. New York: Harper Torchbooks, 1971.

Storey, David. *In Celebration.* London: Hereford Play Series, 1973

——. *The Changing Room, Home, The Contractor.* New York: Avon Books, 1971.

——. *Cromwell.* London: Jonathan Cape, 1973.

——. *The Farm.* London: Samuel French, 1974.

——. *Life Class.* London: Penguin, 1980

——. *The Restoration of Arnold Middleton.* London: Samuel French, 1967

——. *This Sporting Life.* London: Longman, 1960

Strindberg, August. *Miss Julie.* In *Five Plays.* Trans. Harry Carlson. New York: Signet, 1983.

Synge, J. M. *Riders to the Sea.* In *The Playboy of the Western World and Other Plays.* Ed. Ann Saddlemyer. Oxford: Oxford University Press, 1993: 1-12.

Szondi, Peter. *Theory of Modern Drama.* Ed. and trans. Michael Hays. Foreword Jochen Schulte-Sasse. Minneapolis: University of Minnesota Press, 1987.

*Le Théatre, le peuple, la passion* (Discourses and Q&A of Bernard Stiegler, Jean-Christophe Bailly and Denis Guénon). Besançon: Les Solitaires Intempestifs, 2006.

Tocqueville, Alexis de. *Démocracie en Amérique. Oeuvres,* v. 2. Gallimard-Pléiade: Paris, 1992 (orig. pub. 1835 and 1840)

Tolstoy, Leo. *The Power of Darkness.* In *Redemption and Other Plays.* Tr. Arthur Hopkins. New York: Carlton House, nd.

——. *The Realm of Darkness.* In *Plays: Volume Two, 1886-1889.* Intr. Andrew Baruch Wachtel. Tr. Marvin Kantor with Tanya Tulchinsky. Evanstan: Northwestern University Press, 1996.

Turner, Victor. "Frame, Flow and Reflection." *Performance in Postmodern Culture.* Eds. Benamou and Caramello. Madison: Coda Press, 1977.

Turvey, Malcolm. "Balàzs Realist or Modernist?" *October* 115 (Winter, 2006): 77-87

Vinaver, Michel, ed. *Écritures dramatiques: essais d'analyse de textes de théâtre.* Paris: Actes Sud, 1993.

Virilio, Paul. *The Aesthetics of Disappearance.* Trans. Philip Beitchman. New York: Semiotext(e), 1991.

Virno, Paolo. *A Grammar of the Multitude: For an Analysis of Contemporary Forms of Life.* Foreword Sylvère Lotringer. Trans. I. Bertoletti, J. Cascaito, A. Casson. L.A. and N.Y.: Semiotext(e), 2004

——. *Multitude: Between Innovation and Negation.* Trans. I. Bertoletti, J. Cascaito, A. Casson. L.A.: Semiotext(e), 2008.

Waxman, Samuel Montefiore. *Antoine and the Théâtre-Libre.* Cambridge: Harvard University Press, 1926.

Weber, Max. *From Max Weber.* Ed. and trans. H.H. Gerth and C.W. Mills. London: Oxford University Press, 1958.

Weber, Samuel. *Theatricality as Medium.* New York: Fordham University Press, 2004.

Wesker, Arnold. *Love Letters on Blue Paper.* New York: Harper and Row, 1975.

——. *The Plays of Arnold Wesker.* Vol. 1. New York: Harper and Row, 1976.

——. *The Plays of Arnold Wesker.* Vol. 2. New York: Harper and Row, 1977.

Williams, Raymond. *Drama from Ibsen to Brecht.* New York: Oxford University Press, 1971.

Wolin, Sheldon. *Democracy Inc., the Specter of Inverted Totalitarianism.* Princeton: Princeton University Press, 2008.

Wordsworth, William. *"From* Preface to Lyrical Ballads". *Norton Anthology of English Literature: Major Authors Edition.* Ed. Abrams et al. New York: W.W. Norton, 2001: pp. 1436-48.

Zavettino, Cesare. "Some Ideas on Cinema", in *Film: A Montage of Theories.* Ed. R.D. MacCann. New York: Dutton, 1966.

Zinn, Howard. *Failure to Quit.* Monroe, Maine: Common Courage Press, 1993.

Zizek, Slavoj. *Iraq: The Broken Kettle.* London: Verso, 2005.

Zola, Émile. *L'Assomoir.* Paris, 1877.

———. *La Bête humaine.* Ed. and intr. Robert A. Jouanny. Paris: Flammarion, 1972. Orig. published, Paris, 1890.

———. *Le Naturalism au théâtre.* Oeuvres Complètes. Tome 42. Paris, 1927.

———. *L'Oeuvre.* Ed. and intr. Antoinette Ehrard. Paris: Flammarion, 1974. Orig. published, Paris, 1886.

———. *Thérèse Raquin* (play, produced 1873). Oeuvres Complètes. Tome 38. Paris, 1927.

———. *Thérèse Raquin* (novel). Trans. (first published, 1962) Leonard Tancock. London: Penguin, 1987. Orig. pub. Paris, 1867; 2nd ed., with preface (included in above), 1868.

# Index

# Currents in Comparative Romance Languages and Literatures

This series was founded in 1987, and actively solicits book-length manuscripts (approximately 200–400 pages) that treat aspects of Romance languages and literatures. Originally established for works dealing with two or more Romance literatures, the series has broadened its horizons and now includes studies on themes within a single literature or between different literatures, civilizations, art, music, film and social movements, as well as comparative linguistics. Studies on individual writers with an influence on other literatures/civilizations are also welcome. We entertain a variety of approaches and formats, provided the scholarship and methodology are appropriate.

For additional information about the series or for the submission of manuscripts, please contact:

Tamara Alvarez-Detrell and Michael G. Paulson
c/o Dr. Heidi Burns
Peter Lang Publishing, Inc.
P.O. Box 1246
Bel Air, MD 21014-1246

To order other books in this series, please contact our Customer Service Department:

800-770-LANG (within the U.S.)
212-647-7706 (outside the U.S.)
212-647-7707 FAX

or browse online by series at:

www.peterlang.com